PURCHASING AND SUPPLIER INVOLVEMENT: NEW PRODUCT DEVELOPMENT AND PRODUCTION/OPERATIONS PROCESS DEVELOPMENT AND IMPROVEMENT

by

Michael A. McGinnis, D.B.A., C.P.
Professor of Marketing and Lo
University of South Alaban

and

Rafeekh Mele Vallopra
Graduate Research Assistant
University of South Alabama

ACKNOWLEDGMENTS •

This research benefits from the financial support and insights of many institutions and individuals. The Center for Advanced Purchasing Studies provided substantial financial support to fund our efforts during 1996-97. In addition, the University of South Alabama provided a Faculty Service and Development Award in 1997; the support of our department chair, Dr. Grant M. Davis, and dean, Dr. Carl C. Moore, were instrumental in receiving this award. Our colleagues in the Department of Marketing and Transportation absorbed the teaching workload resulting from our assignment to this research. Without this funding and support the research would not have been possible. The reference and interlibrary loan staffs at the University of South Alabama Library were ever ready to respond to our every request.

Early in our research, Professors Gary Ragatz of Michigan State University, William E. Souder of the University of Huntsville, Richard Beltramini of Wayne State University, and Abbie Griffith of the University of Chicago provided background and insights that helped us focus our efforts. Several practitioners provided insight into the new product development process. Mr. Larry Husmann, Director of Corporate Purchasing at Cummins Engines, and Mr. Stephen E. Zimmer, Director of Platforms at Chrysler Corporation, participated in extensive interviews that enabled us to understand supplier involvement from different perspectives.

While many people provided guidance and feedback during questionnaire development we would like to thank the following individuals:
- Mr. Gerard J. (Jerry) Hayes, C.P.M., Denso Manufacturing Michigan, Inc.
- Ms. Dorothy Herold, C.P.M., Motorola, Inc.
- Professor Gary L. Ragatz , Michigan State University
- Mr. Richard G. Weissman, C.P.M., Varian Ion Implant Systems
- Ms. Margaret (Peggy) Williams, C.P.M., Tandem Computers, Inc.

Guidance on the final questionnaires was provided by Dr. Phillip L. Carter, Dr. Richard A. Boyle, and Ms. Carol L. Ketchum of the Center for Advanced Purchasing Studies.

Finally, we would like to thank the hundreds of respondents who took the time to complete our questionnaires. Without their cooperation the results of this study would not have been possible.

To those too numerous to mention who contributed to this research, we offer our appreciation and apologize for not recognizing you individually.

Of course, complete responsibility for the final study rests with the authors of this report.

ISBN: 0-945968-31-0

CONTENTS •

EXHIBITS AND APPENDICES •

PREFACE •

The intentions of this study are to:
- Further the understanding of purchasing and supplier involvement in new product development and process development/improvement
- Develop insights into the relationships among issues that affect new product development and process development/improvement
- Identify managerially useful insights that would be useful to purchasing practitioners in the management of new product development and process development/improvement.

The inspiration for this research is the Center for Advanced Purchasing Studies (CAPS) March 1996 Research Priority #11. This priority is stated as follows: "Early supplier involvement in new product design — Role of purchasing; supplier certification and identification; timing of involvement; technology sharing; monitoring and control; risks/rewards; timesaving quality cost (sic) issues."

In April and May 1996, the authors conducted a literature search to evaluate the feasibility of pursuing CAPS Research Priority #11. The literature review revealed:
1. There is a substantial body of literature on new product development.
2. This body of literature only addresses purchasing's and supplier's roles in new product development.
3. Much of the discussion is normative or based on case studies.
4. A wide range of issues are discussed to provide insights for additional research.
5. The literature does not address all the issues in CAPS Research Priority #11.

In addition, the authors found that the literature placed little emphasis on the processes for producing products. Further literature searches revealed there was little material on purchasing's and supplier's involvement in the development and improvement of production and operations processes. The authors concluded that research into purchasing's and supplier's involvement in both new product development and process development/improvement would be beneficial.

A research proposal was submitted to CAPS in June 1996. The proposal was approved effective beginning September 1996. Two questionnaires were developed: one to address purchasing and supplier involvement in new product development, and another to address purchasing and supplier involvement in process development/improvement.

EXECUTIVE SUMMARY •

BACKGROUND

The research reported in this study addresses purchasing and supplier involvement in new product development and in production or operations process development/improvement. New product development refers *to the procedures that guide the conceptualization, design, engineering, production, and sourcing of a new product. The product may be a good, service, or a combination of both.* Process development/improvement refers to *procedures that guide the conceptualization, design, engineering, manufacturing, and implementation of changes to production/operations processes.* Processes refer to *activities that convert inputs into outputs.*

The purpose of the research reported in this study is to examine the role of suppliers in new product development and in production/operations process development and improvement. While much previous research has focused on new product development, little has been reported of purchasing and supplier efforts to develop and improve the processes for converting inputs (materials and supplies, capital equipment, labor, and information) into products and services.

DESIGN OF THE STUDY

Questionnaire Development

Two questionnaires were developed. The first questionnaire, "Early Supplier Involvement in New Product Development," addressed 10 research issues identified in the CAPS Research Priority #11 and taken from the authors' literature search:

1. Early Supplier Involvement
2. Role of Purchasing
3. Supplier Identification/Certification
4. Timing of Involvement
5. Technology/Information Sharing
6. Monitoring and Control
7. Risk/Reward Sharing
8. Time/Quality/Cost Savings
9. The Business Unit and Its Market
10. Respondent Information

This questionnaire comprised 57 items and was organized into six parts as follows:
- focus of the questionnaire
- purchasing's role in new product development
- the supplier's role in new product development
- practices regarding supplier involvement in new product development
- competitive environment
- general information.

Three letters were prepared to encourage subject response. A prenotification letter was mailed one week in advance of the questionnaire, a cover letter accompanied the questionnaire, and a follow-up letter was mailed one week after the questionnaire mailing.

The second questionnaire, "Purchasing Involvement in Production Process Development and Improvement," addressed 11 research issues adopted from the first questionnaire:

1. Supplier Involvement in Process Development/Improvement
2. Role of Purchasing
3. Supplier Identification/Certification
4. Timing of Involvement
5. Technology Sharing
6. Monitoring and Control
7. Risk/Rewards
8. Time/Quality/Cost Savings
9. Importance of Process Development/Improvement Relative to New Product Development
10. The Business Unit and Its Market
11. Respondent Information

This questionnaire comprised 48 items and was organized into six parts as follows:
- focus of the questionnaire
- processes in your business unit
- purchasing's role in process development/improvement
- the supplier's role in process development/improvement
- competitive environment
- general information

Three letters were prepared to encourage subject response. A prenotification letter was mailed one week in advance of the questionnaire, a cover letter accompanied the questionnaire, and a follow-up letter was mailed one week after the questionnaire mailing.

Sampling

The questionnaires were mailed to senior purchasing managers who were members of the National Association of Purchasing Management and had addresses in the United States. Two random samples were drawn without replacement.

The new product development questionnaire was sent to 1,074 individuals. Two hundred seventy-one usable responses were returned, for a response rate of 25.2 percent. The process development and improvement was mailed to 1,051 individuals. Two hundred fifty-two usable responses were returned, for a response rate of 24.0 percent.

Data Analysis

Data analysis focused on (a) developing constructs that explain data, (b) examining the effects of the research issues on new product success (in the first questionnaire), and (c) examining the effects of the research issues on process as a source of competitive advantage (in the second questionnaire).

SUMMARY OF STUDY A: PURCHASING AND SUPPLIER INVOLVEMENT IN NEW PRODUCT DEVELOPMENT

Purchasing and Supplier Issues That Are Essential to New Product Success

This research identified three managerial variables essential to new product success:
- the business unit's orientation to time competitiveness
- the thoroughness of the decision-making process of whether or not to include suppliers in new product development
- purchasing's role in new product development.

The authors conclude that if the following primary issues are not addressed effectively, other issues of purchasing and supplier involvement in new product development will not realize their full potential, nor will they compensate for lapses in the essential managerial variables:

1. Whether or not suppliers are involved in new product development, the organization's attitude toward time competitiveness will affect new product success. If suppliers are not involved in new product development, this is the only essential managerial variable identified in this study that contributes to product success.

2. If suppliers are involved in new product development, a combination of (a) careful evaluation of whether or not suppliers can contribute to new product objectives, and (b) close coordination and careful control of the efforts of selected suppliers is also essential to new product success.

3. If suppliers are involved in new product development, new product success will be enhanced if purchasing has a significant new product development role. This role includes early involvement in new product development, proactive participation in cross-functional teams, and active participation in identifying high-potential suppliers.

If suppliers are not involved in new product development, purchasing will be important, but not essential, to new product success. The absence of supplier involvement appears to decrease the importance of purchasing's integrative role in new product development.

Purchasing and Supplier Issues That Are Important to New Product Success

This research also identified three managerial variables, one outcome, and one external environmental variable that are important, yet not essential, to new product success. The authors believe these secondary elements are most effective when the essential requirements for new product success are present. In their absence, the following issues will not achieve their potential for contributing to new product success:

1. The first managerial variable is *Continuing New Product Development Commitment.* This variable includes five components. They are (a) shared education and training, (b) shared plant and equipment, (c) co-location of buyer and supplier personnel, (d) formalized risk/reward sharing agreements, and (e) training in mutual trust development. Taken together, these five components create a framework for continuing cooperation.

2. The second managerial variable is *Explicit New Product Development Processes.* This variable focuses on the operational aspects of selecting and integrating suppliers into new product development programs. Two components of this managerial variable recognize the need to have formal processes for selecting suppliers once a decision has been made to involve suppliers in new product development. One of the components acknowledge the need for explicit agreements to establish the rules of involvement. The final two components formalize the interactive nature of supplier involvement in new product development.

Notice that this managerial variable operationalizes the vision of mutual cooperation often mentioned in the literature.

3. The third managerial variable is *Sharing Confidential Information.* This frequent sharing of customer, product, and process technical information indicates the extent to which buyer and suppliers communicate when involved in new product development.

4. One outcome, *Supplier Integration,* was identified as being important to new product success. The components of this outcome focus on new product time-to-market and quality. According to the results, supplier integration enhances time-to-market and product quality.

5. The environmental variable, *Competitive Market Hostility,* was associated with product success. Apparently, the perception of hostile and competitive market creates superordinate goals that provide the motivation to develop products that are successful.

Other Considerations

1. Purchasing and supplier involvement can have an impact on new product success in both manufacturing and service industry categories. Although the estimated response rate in non-manufacturing industry categories was lower, the effect of purchasing and supplier involvement on new product success did not differ from manufacturing respondents.

2. Purchasing and supplier involvement in new product development were not affected by country of ownership, respondent experience, or respondent professional certification.

Research Issues: Overall Findings

Careful examination of the results did not reveal significant findings beyond those previously discussed. However, those findings can be restated in the context of the research issues as follows:

1. The business unit's competitive responsiveness is essential to new product success regardless of whether suppliers are involved in new product development or not.
2. Although purchasing's role is essential to new product success when suppliers are involved in new product development, it is also important when suppliers are not involved.
3. Supplier identification and certification are important to new product success; however, careful evaluation of whether or not to use suppliers is essential to new product success when suppliers are involved.
4. The timing of supplier involvement in new

product development does not affect new product success.
5. Supplier monitoring and control are important, but not essential, to new product success.
6. Risk/reward sharing is important, but not essential, to new product success.
7. New product success in terms of sales, profits, time-to-market and quality are improved by supplier involvement in new product development.

SUMMARY OF STUDY B: PURCHASING AND SUPPLIER INVOLVEMENT IN PROCESS DEVELOPMENT AND IMPROVEMENT

Process as a Source of Competitive Advantage

Processes are an important source of competitive advantage (low cost, meaningful differentiation, or both). The level of importance is comparable to that of new product development as a source of competitive advantage. This conclusion does not imply any inherent conflict between these two priorities; however, emphasis on one at the expense of the other may be detrimental to overall business unit success. In many instances process development/improvement and new product development will occur concurrently.

Purchasing management and staff must be aware of the potential for their contribution to both process development/improvement and new product development success.

The Role of Purchasing in Process Development/Improvement

Purchasing plays a major role in process development/improvement in over 80 percent of the respondents' business units. This role includes constant involvement, taking a proactive role in cross-functional teams, and actively seeking to identify technology that is important to process development/improvement.

The Role of Supplier in Process Development/Improvement

Suppliers play a major role in process development/improvement in nearly 75 percent of the respondents' business units. Supplier participation contributes to competitive advantage in the areas of new product time-to-market, higher quality, and cost savings.

Supplier Management in Process Development/Improvement

Supplier management in process development/improvement focuses more on the identification of important technology and suppliers and on coordination than it does on supplier selection and control. This may be because process development/improvement for new and existing products is an ongoing process.

Industry Considerations

Process development/improvement offers the potential for competitive advantage in manufacturing, service, and other industry categories. Purchasing and supplier involvement in process development/improvement are substantial in all three industry categories.

Other Considerations

Country of ownership, respondent experience, and respondent certification did not affect purchasing or supplier involvement in process development/improvement. The study of purchasing and supplier involvement in process development/improvement warrants additional attention from academic researchers, practitioners, and the trade press.

Research Issues: Overall Findings

Careful examination of the results did not reveal significant findings beyond those previously stated; however, those findings can be restated in the context of the research issues as follows:

1. Production/operations process development and improvement is a source of competitive advantage (low cost, meaningful differentiation, or both) to business units in manufacturing, service, and other industry categories.
2. Purchasing plays an important role in process development/improvement whether or not suppliers are involved. This occurs in all industry categories.
3. Supplier involvement in process development/ improvement is common in all three industry categories.
4. In process development/improvement, the identification of technology and suppliers is important. Because suppliers are frequently involved, the evaluation of whether or not to use suppliers in process development/improvement projects does not appear to be a concern.
5. The timing of supplier involvement in process development/improvement does not affect outcomes. The best time to involve suppliers varies with the situation.
6. In supplier management, coordination is more important in process development/implementation than is supplier selection and control.
7. The importance of process development/ improvement to business unit competitive advantage is comparable to the importance of new product development.

8. While business unit competitive responsiveness and external environmental competitive hostility are associated with the perceived importance of process as a source of competitive advantage, they do not motivate purchasing or supplier involvement in process development/improvement.

IMPLICATIONS AND CONCLUSIONS

Purchasing's Role in New Product Development

The traditional role of purchasing as a transaction processor has changed. The need for purchasing to contribute to organizational success is well established. According to the results of this research, purchasing can contribute to organizational success by increasing its contributions to new product development. Three elements are essential to this participation: early involvement in new product development programs, good cross-functional team skills, and the ability to identify useful suppliers.

Purchasing's early involvement in new product development programs will increase as a result of management directive, business unit policy, purchasing initiative, or a combination of the three.

The development of cross-functional team skills includes learning to participate in and lead teams that are diverse in terms of education, job assignment, job level, gender, race, and individual personality. Diverse teams may also include suppliers representatives. In many teams, purchasing personnel may assume a leadership role in some situations, and a support role at other times.

A wide range of individual abilities are important in the development of team skills. These include effective listening and negotiations, time management, planning, and conflict resolution. Purchasing personnel should also have the ability to understand and work with other business functions.

The development of team skills is a shared responsibility of general management, purchasing management, and the individual. Without the support of general management, the potential accomplishments of the department and its individuals will be limited. However, the lack of management commitment should not completely preclude individual development. Effective team skills in purchasing can contribute to overall effectiveness even when the organizational environment is not team oriented.

Being able to identify suppliers that can contribute to new product development requires that purchasing assume a proactive role toward the process of supplier development. Topics for identifying new suppliers are discussed in many purchasing text books, C.P.M. and

A.P.P. study materials, and trade publications. The process of supplier development has become more sophisticated as personal computers and software have become less expensive.

Supplier Involvement in New Product Development

Three issues are essential to effective supplier involvement in new product development: supplier evaluation, control, and coordination; an organizational culture that responds quickly and effectively to challenges; and substantial purchasing involvement in new product development.

Evaluation, control, and coordination involve three key issues:

a. Careful evaluation by the business unit to decide whether quality, time, and cost objectives can best be achieved internally or by working with a supplier

b. Control of supplier integration into the new product development process by the buyer

c. Close coordination of all facets of supplier integration objectives including quality, time-to-market, and cost goals

Organizational competitive responsiveness includes the ability to respond quickly and effectively to changing customer needs, changing competitor strategies, and the ability to effectively bring new products to market faster than competitors. Apparently, the business unit's competitive responsiveness provides motivation that leads to a higher proportion of successful new products.

When significantly involved in new product development, purchasing contributes to the decision of whether or not to include suppliers in new product development, the identification of suppliers that can offer needed technologies, the ability to contribute early in new product development, and the ability to work effectively in cross-functional teams. Effective purchasing involvement also contributes to control, coordination, and evaluation.

According to the research, effective integration, once an organization has decided to use suppliers in new product or process development, includes at least eight issues:

a. shared education and training programs

b. co-location of supplier and buyer personnel

c. shared physical assets (plant and equipment)

d. formalized risk/reward sharing agreements

e. supplier participation in buyer project teams

f. direct cross-functional, intercompany communication

g. formal buyer procedures for selecting suppliers to be integrated into programs

h. sharing of technical information and customer requirements with suppliers on a continuing, as-needed basis

Purchasing's Role in Process Development/Improvement

As stated earlier, the role of purchasing and purchasing's contribution to organizational success is well established. According to the results of this research, purchasing can contribute to organizational success through early involvement in production and operations process development and improvement. Four factors are essential to this involvement:
- a willingness to participate early in process development/improvement programs
- good cross-functional team skills
- the ability to identify useful suppliers
- the ability to identify useful technology

As discussed earlier, purchasing's early involvement in new product development programs will increase as a result of management directive, business unit policy, purchasing initiative, or a combination of the three. Effective purchasing involvement in process development/improvement also requires that purchasing personnel have the ability to identify promising process technology. This ability requires that purchasing have a greater level of familiarity with the inputs, processes, and outputs of the business unit. For example, a working knowledge of hazardous waste regulations would be beneficial to a purchasing professional looking for technology applicable to processes in a chemical plant. For purchasing managers and staff seeking promising technology, the necessary expertise could be gained from increased coordination with engineering and technical staff, from formal training, or by working with cross-functional teams. In some instances, a desirable approach would be to recruit purchasing staff with the necessary technological skills from other functions in the organization or from college/university programs that provide the necessary technological training.

Supplier Involvement in Process Development/Improvement

Three issues important to effective supplier involvement in process development/improvement include suppler control and coordination, openness to supplier ideas, and substantial purchasing involvement in process development/improvement.

Supplier control and coordination include two key issues:

a. Control of supplier integration into the new product/ process development process by the buyer

b. Close coordination of all facets of supplier integration objectives including quality, time-to-market, and cost goals

As discussed earlier, when significantly involved in new product development, purchasing contributes to the identification of suppliers that can offer needed technology, the ability to contribute early in process development/improvement, and the ability to work effectively in cross-functional teams. Effective purchasing involvement also contributes to supplier control and coordination.

Similarities of Purchasing/Supplier Involvement in New Product Development and in Process Development/Improvement

First, early and extensive involvement of purchasing contributes to new product development and process development/improvement success. This is especially true when suppliers are involved. This role includes early involvement, effective participation in cross-functional teams, and supplier identification in both situations.

Second, business unit control and coordination are important to successful integration of suppliers in new product and process projects. This includes close cooperation, joint setting of goals, measurement, and integration of suppliers into projects.

Next, the organization's orientation to time competitiveness affects both new product and process programs. A business unit's emphasis on quick and effective responsiveness to customer needs and competitor strategies, together with the ability to bring new products quickly and effectively to market, are common to both successful new product and process projects.

Fourth, the timing of supplier involvement, whether before or after the concept stage, does not affect new product or process project success. The timing of supplier involvement is unique to each situation.

Finally, although supplier involvement in new product development and in process development/improvement occurs more often in manufacturing, however, supplier involvement is not uncommon in the service and other industry categories.

Differences between Purchasing/Supplier Involvement in New Product Development and in Process Development/Improvement

Purchasing involvement in new product development emphasizes the identification of suppliers. Purchasing involvement in process development/improvement includes identifying important technology as well as important suppliers. In process development/improvement less emphasis appears to be put on the evaluation of whether or not to use suppliers than on new product development. This could be because process development/improvement is an ongoing process. While the sharing of facilities, training, and physical assets affected new product success, this consideration was not addressed in the process development/improvement study. Further research is needed to determine the effect of sharing on process development/improvement. Finally, the role of the business unit's external environment does not seem to play an important role in process development/improvement.

Similarities and Differences in Perspective

The differences between purchasing and supplier involvement in new product development and process development/improvement appear to be relatively minor as compared to the similarities. This suggests that skills contributing to effective purchasing and supplier involvement in one of these activities can contribute to effective involvement in the other. These similarities also suggest that developmental programs designed to enhance purchasing and/or supplier involvement are likely to be applicable to both new product development and process development/improvement programs. Finally, these similarities suggest that purchasing should be aware of potential contributions to the business unit's new products and processes. The emphasis on either product or on processes to the exclusion of the other may result in missed opportunities for contributions to business unit competitive advantage.

SELF-CRITIQUE EXERCISES

Based on the results of this research, two self-critique exercises were developed. The purpose of these exercises is to enable the purchasing executive or manager to evaluate purchasing and supplier involvement in new product development and process development/improvement in his/her organization. One self-critique exercise focuses on purchasing and supplier involvement in new product development. The other exercise focuses on purchasing and supplier involvement in production/operations process development/improvement. Both exercises are presented in this report's Self-Critique Exercises section.

RECOMMENDATIONS FOR FURTHER RESEARCH

Several topics raised during completion of this report warrant further study:

1. The replication of Study A and Study B at a later date should provide insights into both the changing roles of purchasing and supplier involvement in new product development and process development/improvement.

2. Further research into the roles of purchasing and of suppliers would provide additional insights into policies and procedures that aid in process development/improvement project success.

3. Further research would provide additional insights into the role of organizational priorities on purchasing and supplier involvement in new product development and process development/improvement.

4. Further research could examine the roles of purchasing and supplier involvement in new product development and process development/improvement in service industries.

IMPLICATIONS FOR THE PRACTITIONER •

This section emphasizes applications of this research for purchasing practitioners at the managerial and executive levels. This section is organized into four parts:

- How the results of Study A, Purchasing and Supplier Involvement in New Product Development, can be applied to tactical and strategic purchasing management.
- How the results of Study B, Purchasing and Supplier Involvement in Process Development and Improvement, can be applied to tactical and strategic purchasing management.
- Compare/contrast insights from the two studies.
- Introduce two self-critique exercises.

One exercise is for those interested in evaluating purchasing and supplier involvement in new product development in their business unit. The other is for those who want to critique purchasing and supplier involvement in process development and improvement.

PURCHASING AND SUPPLIER INVOLVEMENT IN NEW PRODUCT DEVELOPMENT

Purchasing's Role

The traditional role of purchasing as a transaction processor has changed. The need for purchasing to contribute to organizational success is well established. According to the results of this research, purchasing can contribute to organizational success by increasing its contributions to new product development. Three elements are essential to this participation: early involvement in new product development programs, good cross-functional team skills, and the ability to identify useful suppliers.

Purchasing's early involvement in new product development programs will increase as a result of management directive, business unit policy, purchasing initiative, or a combination of the three.

The development of cross-functional team skills includes learning to participate in and lead teams that are diverse in terms of education, job assignment, job level, gender, race, and individual personality. Diverse teams may also include supplier representatives. In many teams, purchasing personnel may assume a leadership role in some situations, and a support role at other times.

A wide range of individual abilities are important in the development of team skills. These include effective listening and negotiations, time management, planning, and conflict resolution. Purchasing personnel should also have the ability to understand and work with other business functions.

The development of team skills is a shared responsibility of general management, purchasing management, and the individual. Without the support of general management, the potential accomplishments of the department and its individuals will be limited. However, the lack of management commitment should not completely preclude individual development. Effective team skills in purchasing can contribute to overall effectiveness even when the organizational environment is not team oriented.

Being able to identify suppliers that can contribute to new product development requires that purchasing assume a proactive role towards the process of supplier development. Topics for identifying new suppliers are discussed in many purchasing text books, C.P.M., and A.P.P. study materials, and trade publications. The process of supplier development has become more sophisticated as personal computers and software have become less expensive.

Supplier Involvement

Three issues are essential to effective supplier involvement in new product development: supplier evaluation, control, and coordination; an organizational culture that responds quickly and effectively to challenges; and substantial purchasing involvement in new product development.

Evaluation, control, and coordination involve three key issues:

a. Careful evaluation by the business unit to decide whether quality, time, and cost objectives can best be achieved internally or by working with a supplier

b. Control of supplier integration into the new product development process by the buyer

c. Close coordination of all facets of supplier integration objectives including quality, time-to-market, and cost goals

Organizational competitive responsiveness includes the ability to respond quickly and effectively to changing customer needs, changing competitor strategies, and the ability to effectively bring new products to market faster than competitors. Apparently, the business unit's competitive responsiveness provides motivation that leads to a higher proportion of successful new products.

When significantly involved in new product development, purchasing contributes to the decision of whether or not to include suppliers in new product development, the identification of suppliers that can offer needed technologies, the ability to contribute early in new product development, and the ability to work effectively in cross-functional teams. Effective purchasing involvement also contributes to control, coordination, and evaluation.

According to the research, effective integration, once an organization has decided to use suppliers in new product or process development, includes at least eight issues:

   a. shared education and training programs

   b. co-location of supplier and buyer personnel

   c. shared physical assets (plant and equipment)

   d. formalized risk/reward sharing agreements

   e. supplier participation in buyer project teams

   f. direct cross-functional, intercompany communications

   g. formal buyer procedures for selecting suppliers to be integrated into programs

   h. sharing of technical information and customer requirements with suppliers on a continuing, as-needed basis

PURCHASING AND SUPPLIER INVOLVEMENT IN PROCESS DEVELOPMENT/IMPROVEMENT

Purchasing's Role

As stated earlier, the role of purchasing and purchasing's contribution to organizational success is well established. According to the results of this research, purchasing can contribute to organizational success through early involvement in production and operations process development and improvement. Four factors are essential to this involvement:
   • a willingness to participate early in process development/improvement programs
   • good cross-functional team skills
   • the ability to identify useful suppliers
   • the ability to identify useful technology

Purchasing's early involvement in new product development programs will increase as a result of management

directive, business unit policy, purchasing initiative, or a combination of the three. Effective purchasing involvement in process development/improvement also requires that purchasing personnel have the ability to identify promising process technology.

This ability requires that purchasing have a greater level of familiarity with the inputs, processes, and outputs of the business unit. For example, a working knowledge of hazardous waste regulations would be beneficial to a purchasing professional looking for technology applicable to processes in a chemical plant. For purchasing managers and staff seeking promising technology, the necessary expertise could be gained from increased coordination with engineering and technical staff, from formal training, or by working with cross-functional teams. In some instances, a desirable approach would be to recruit purchasing staff with the necessary technological skills from other functions in the organization or from college/university programs that provide the necessary technological training.

Supplier Involvement

Three issues important to effective supplier involvement in process development/improvement include supplier control and coordination openness to supplier ideas and substantial purchasing involvement in process development/improvement.

Supplier control and coordination include two key issues:

   a. Control of supplier integration into the new product/process development process by the buyer

   b. Close coordination of all facets of supplier integration objectives including quality, time-to-market, and cost goals

As discussed earlier, when significantly involved in new product development, purchasing contributes to the identification suppliers that can offer needed technology, the ability to contribute early in process development/improvement, and the ability to work effectively in cross-functional teams. Effective purchasing involvement also contributes to supplier control and coordination.

COMPARISON AND CONTRAST: PURCHASING AND SUPPLIER INVOLVEMENT IN NEW PRODUCT DEVELOPMENT AND PROCESS DEVELOPMENT/IMPROVEMENT

Although there are many similarities between purchasing/supplier involvement in new product development and process development improvement, some differences do exist.

Similarities

First, early and extensive involvement of purchasing contributes to new product development and process development/improvement success. This is especially true when suppliers are involved. This role includes early involvement, effective participation in cross-functional teams, and supplier identification in both situations.

Second, business unit control and coordination are important to successful integration of suppliers in new product and process projects. This includes close cooperation, joint setting of goals, measurement, and integration of suppliers into projects.

Next, the organization's orientation to time competitiveness affects both new product and process programs. A business unit's emphasis on quick and effective responsiveness to customer needs and competitor strategies, together with the ability to bring new products quickly and effectively to market, are common to both successful new product and process projects.

Fourth, the timing of supplier involvement, whether before or after the concept stage, does not affect new product or process project success. The timing of supplier involvement is unique to each situation.

Finally, although supplier involvement in new product development and in process development/improvement occurs more often in manufacturing, supplier involvement is not uncommon in the service and other industry categories.

Differences

Purchasing involvement in new product development emphasizes the identification of suppliers. Purchasing involvement in process development/improvement includes identifying important technology as well as important suppliers. In process development/improvement less emphasis appears to be put on the evaluation of whether or not to use suppliers than on new product development. This could be because process development/improvement is an ongoing process. While the sharing of facilities, training, and physical assets affected new product success, this consideration was not addressed in the process development/improvement study. Further research is needed to determine the effect of sharing on process development/improvement. Finally, the role of the business unit's external environment does not seem to play an important role in process development/improvement.

Similarities and Differences in Perspective

The differences between purchasing and supplier involvement in new product development and process development/improvement appear to be relatively minor as compared to the similarities. This suggests that skills contributing to effective purchasing and supplier involvement in one of these activities can contribute to effective involvement in the other. These similarities also suggest that developmental programs designed to enhance purchasing and/or supplier involvement are likely to be applicable to both new product development and process development/improvement programs. Finally, these similarities suggest that purchasing should be aware of potential contributions to the business unit's new products and processes. The emphasis on either product or on processes to the exclusion of the other may result in missed opportunities for contributions to business unit competitive advantage.

SELF-CRITIQUE EXERCISES

Based on the results of this research, two self-critique exercises were developed. The purpose of these exercises is to enable the purchasing executive or manager to evaluate purchasing and supplier involvement in new product development and process development/improvement in his/her organization. One self-critique exercise focuses on purchasing and supplier involvement in new product development. The other exercise focuses on purchasing and supplier involvement in production/operations process development/improvement. Both exercises are presented in this report's Self-Critique Exercises section.

DESIGN OF THE STUDY •

INTRODUCTION

The focus of this research is early supplier involvement in new product design. Topics include the role of purchasing; supplier identification and certification; timing of involvement; technology sharing; monitoring and control; risks/rewards; and timesaving, quality, and cost issues.

An extensive literature review was undertaken beginning in the spring of 1996. The authors found that a great deal of literature focused on new product development. This literature reported the results of a wide range of studies using an array of research methodologies including case studies, field interviews, structured and open-ended surveys, and literature reviews. While substantial literature on new product development had developed, the relationships among new product development, purchasing's role, and supplier involvement were not well integrated. (An annotated bibliography is included in this report as an appendix.)

During the literature search the authors observed that very little had been published regarding production and operations process development and improvement. The authors believed that process improvements are a source of competitive advantage (low cost producer, meaningful differentiation, or both) for new and mature products. As a result of their study and teaching of purchasing, the authors appreciated the importance of cost reduction and efficiency increases that result from process improvements. Further investigation confirmed that little had been published to date regarding process improvement in the academic literature and trade press.

QUESTIONNAIRE DEVELOPMENT

After reviewing time, cost, and sample-size considerations, the authors developed two structured mail questionnaires. One questionnaire focused on new product development while the other focused on production and operations process development and improvement. The new product development questionnaire was created first.

Development of the New Product Development Questionnaire

Based on a review of CAPS Research Priority #11 and the literature survey, 10 research issues were identified:

1. Early Supplier Involvement
2. Role of Purchasing
3. Supplier Identification/Certification
4. Timing of Involvement
5. Technology/Information Sharing
6. Monitoring and Control
7. Risk/Reward Sharing
8. Time/Quality Savings
9. The Business Unit and Its Market
10. Respondent Information

Items were written and organized into a draft questionnaire. This draft questionnaire was pretested with selected practitioners, academics, and members of CAPS' staff. The questionnaire was then finalized, and prenotification, cover, and follow-up letters were prepared. The questionnaire and letters are shown in Appendix II.

Development of the Process Development and Improvement Questionnaire

Based on further review of CAPS Research Priority #11, the findings of the literature, and a review of the new product development questionnaire, 11 research issues were identified:

1. Early Supplier Involvement
2. Role of Purchasing
3. Supplier Identification/Certification
4. Timing of Involvement
5. Technology Sharing
6. Monitoring and Control
7. Risk/Reward Sharing
8. Time/Quality/Cost Savings
9. Importance of Process Development/Improvement Relative to New Product Development
10. The Business Unit and Its Market
11. Respondent Information

Items were written and organized into a draft questionnaire. This draft questionnaire was pretested with selected practitioners and members of CAPS' staff. The questionnaire was then finalized, and prenotification, cover, and follow-up letters were prepared. The questionnaire and letters are shown in Appendix II.

SAMPLING

A discussion of subjects for the research concluded that the population sampled should consist of individuals familiar with purchasing from a managerial to executive level. The National Association of Purchasing Management's "Title 1" (purchasing senior management) mailing list was available. This list included approximately 3,500 members of the National Association of Purchasing Management representing a variety of industry categories.

Rather than focus on a limited number of industry categories (roughly corresponding to Standard Industrial Classification Codes), the authors studied purchasing and supplier involvement across industry categories.

The mailing list was divided into 10 subgroups of approximately equal size. Random sampling without replacement was used to select the subjects for the research. As a result, no individual participated in both studies. Samples of 1,054 and 1,074 individuals were drawn for the first and second questionnaires respectively.

The new product development questionnaire was mailed in February 1997. The production process development/improvement questionnaire was mailed in March 1997.

DATA ANALYSIS

For each study questionnaires were screened for completeness of response and coded. For each questionnaire, items within each section were factor analyzed to identify constructs underlying the responses in that section. The statistical package used for this analysis was SPSS for Microsoft Windows 6.2. A Varimax Rotation was used to maximize the internal similarity of factors and minimize the similarity among or between factors within a questionnaire section.

Factor scores were computed for each individual by summing the factor items and dividing by the number of items loading on the factor. The factor scores were used as input for subsequent analysis. Respondents were then divided into "high" and "low" categories based on their mean factor scores.

Three statistical techniques were used to assess the relationships in the data. The t-test was used to test for differences between means when the subjects had been divided into two categories. The level of significance used in all statistical tests was 0.05. Then, multiple regression analysis was used to assess the relative importance of the variables identified as significant in the t-test. The third statistical technique used in the data analysis was contingency table analysis with the chi-square statistic. This nonparametric test is used when nominally scaled.

RESULTS

Data analysis outputs were examined for significant differences between or among variables. Results were reported and summarized. Inspection of results summaries led to the conclusions reported in the studies. Further examination of conclusions resulted in the preparation of insights for practitioners and the development of two self-critique exercises for use by purchasing practitioners.

STUDY A: PURCHASING AND SUPPLIER INVOLVEMENT IN NEW PRODUCT DEVELOPMENT •

INTRODUCTION

This study examines purchasing and supplier involvement in new product development with emphasis on the role played by suppliers. Study B examines purchasing and supplier involvement in production/operations process improvement and development. In this study, *new product development was defined as new products being marketed by the business unit to consumers, industrial customers, and/or resellers.* The new product development process was defined as *procedures that guide the conceptualization, design, engineering, production, and sourcing of a new product.* A product could be a good, service, or a combination of both.

Eight specific issues were addressed in the research on purchasing and supplier involvement in new product development:

1. Role of Purchasing

2. Supplier Identification/Certification

3. Timing of Involvement

4. Technology/Information Sharing

5. Monitoring and Control

6. Risk/Reward Sharing

7. Time/Quality/Cost Savings

8. The Business Unit and Its Market

A detailed statistical analysis of responses to the questionnaire used to address these issues appears as Appendix III. This chapter is organized into six sections. The following sections discuss the factors, or concepts, identified in this study and relate these factors to the contributions of purchasing and suppliers to new product success. Next, the results of the factor analysis are analyzed to develop insights regarding purchasing and supplier contributions to new product success. The third section briefly discusses the affect of business unit ownership, industry category, business unit size, and respondent qualifications on perceived product success.

Next, the affect of business unit ownership, industry category, business unit size, and respondent qualifications on supplier participation in new product development are discussed. The fifth section focuses on the eight research issues and discusses their implications for purchasing. The final section presents the conclusions of the study.

THE DIMENSIONS OF PURCHASING AND SUPPLIER INVOLVEMENT IN NEW PRODUCT DEVELOPMENT

A statistical data reduction technique, called *factor analysis,* was used to simplify questionnaire responses. An examination of the reliability of the results identified 11 factors used to explain the involvement of purchasing and suppliers in new product development. Each identified factor, or concept, consists of two or more component statements that relate to the research issues.

A description of these 11 factors and their components follows, and the relationship between these factors and the research issues is discussed. The alpha-numeric identification of the factors represents sections of the questionnaire. Only factors with an adequate level of reliability are discussed.

Factor B-1: Purchasing Plays a Major Role in the New Product Development Process

Five questionnaire items comprise this factor. They indicate a "major purchasing role in new product development" includes purchasing (a) becoming involved in the new product development process at the concept stage, (b) taking a leadership role in new product development cross-functional teams, and (c) identifying suppliers that offer competitive technology.

A wide range of skills and abilities are needed for purchasing to play a major role in new product development. These include (a) an overall awareness of the firm, its strategies, and objectives, (b) a working knowledge of the technology and processes used in the firm's new product development process, (c) good working relationships with other departments, (d) strong interpersonal and leadership skills within the purchasing department, (e) familiarity with existing suppliers, and (f) an awareness of the potentials of existing and prospective suppliers.

In order for purchasing to play a major role in new product development an audit of purchasing would be desirable. The five questionnaire items identified with the "Purchasing in a New Product Development Role" concept provide a starting point for such an audit. Five questions that can provide insight into purchasing's new product development role are as follows:

1. Does purchasing play a major role in the new product development process?
2. Does purchasing become involved in the new product development process at the concept stage?
3. Does purchasing play an important role in new product development cross-functional teams?
4. Does purchasing take a leadership role in new product development cross-functional teams?
5. Does purchasing play an important role in identifying suppliers offering technology that can provide the organization with a competitive advantage?

Answers of yes to these five questions suggest the purchasing department is positioned to contribute to new product development. Answers of no to any of these questions suggest there may be room for improvement in purchasing's capabilities. Further evaluation of the purchasing department's policies, management, and staff should identify areas for development or change.

Factor B-2: New Product Success

This factor is an outcome of effective new product development. The three outcomes identified are meeting or exceeding (a) sales objectives, (b) profit objectives, and (c) time-to-market schedule. The focal question for purchasing management is: How can purchasing and/or supplier involvement in the new product development process contribute to achieving or exceeding sales, profit, and time-to-market objectives? Identifying how purchasing and suppliers can contribute to these three objectives is a good starting point for determining what role purchasing and suppliers should play in new product development, what capabilities they possess, and what capabilities they need to develop.

Factor C-1: New Product Development Strategic Evaluation and Control

This factor demonstrates a key interactive role played by purchasing to successfully involve suppliers in new product development. Purchasing contributes in two ways. First, it contributes to decisions regarding whether or not to use suppliers in new product development. Three components address this concern: (a) careful evaluation of whether new technology is better developed by the buyer or with a supplier, (b) careful evaluation of whether time-to-market objectives can best be met by the buyer or with a supplier, and (c) careful evaluation of whether new product quality objectives can best be met by the buyer or with a supplier.

Second, purchasing contributes to the process of coordinating and integrating supplier participation in new product development. Three components address this concern: (a) close coordination of supplier efforts with the new product development process, (b) control of supplier integration into the new product development process, and (c) working closely with suppliers to achieve specific objectives.

This factor raises two questions that purchasing management must consider:

1. Does purchasing have the skills and resources needed to contribute to evaluation processes that determine whether a new product development program should include suppliers?
2. Does purchasing have the skills and resources needed to contribute to the integration of suppliers in the new product development process?

Answers of yes to these questions suggest purchasing is not only positioned to contribute to the process of deciding whether to use suppliers but also contribute to the successful integration of suppliers when they are used. Answers of no to either of these questions indicate purchasing is not in a position to effectively contribute to supplier participation in new product development.

Factor C-2: Suppliers in a Major New Product Development Role

This factor provides a means for assessing whether or not suppliers play an important role in new product development. While subjective in nature, the responses to the three questionnaire items addressing this concept provide a means of assessing the extent of supplier involvement in new product development. The combination of important role, frequent use, and early involvement identify the concept as perceived by the research respondents.

This factor provides a means for purchasing managers to assess the extent to which suppliers are involved in new product development. Three questions can be used as a means of assessing supplier involvement:

1. When involved, do suppliers play an important role in new product development?
2. Are suppliers involved frequently in new product development?
3. When involved, are suppliers included in new product development at the concept stage?

Answers of yes to these questions suggest suppliers are involved in a major new product development role.

Answers of yes to questions 1 and 3, and an answer of no to question 2 indicate suppliers play an important role on a selective basis. While supplier involvement is not necessarily a panacea for everyone's new product development needs, these answers should raise the additional question: *Can we effectively involve suppliers more often in new product development?*

An answer of yes to question 2, and answers of no to questions 1 and 3 indicate that suppliers are involved in a minor role. This pattern of answers should raise the question: *Will greater supplier involvement contribute to our new product development?*

An answer of no to all three questions indicates minimal supplier involvement in new product development. Two follow-up questions to these answers are: *Are there good reasons why suppliers are not involved in new product development? and Are we missing opportunities by not involving suppliers in new product development?*

In some cases more frequent and/or greater supplier involvement will improve new product development. The point here is not that supplier involvement in new product development is desirable for its own sake; rather, these questions should be asked, and answered, in the context of your business unit's needs.

Factor C-3: Supplier Integration New Product Development Outcomes

This factor measures the outcome of supplier integration into new product development. The two outcomes are reduced time-to-market and higher product quality. Insights from this factor may be used by purchasing for post hoc analysis of supplier involvement in new product development. Specific questions based on this factor would be: *Did supplier involvement reduce new product time-to-market? and Did supplier involvement result in higher new product quality?* The answers to these questions might (a) lead to insights that improve suppliers' contributions to new product development, or (b) help evaluate whether continued supplier involvement can contribute to new product development.

Factor C-5: Timing of Supplier New Product Development Involvement

This factor provides a means of evaluating the timing of supplier involvement in new product development. This factor helps to ascertain whether or not the actual timing of supplier involvement affects new product success.

The next three factors were based on previous research identifying variables that differed between successful and unsuccessful new product development projects. The purpose of the factor analysis was to identify groupings of these issues that represented common constructs and evaluate whether or not these constructs were associated with new product success. These factors provide purchasing management with techniques that can be useful for evaluating and managing supplier involvement in new product development. The following sections discuss these factors and suggest how they might be used in the process of managing supplier involvement in new product development.

Factor D-1: Continuing New Product Development Commitment

Five issues in this factor describe the dimensions of buyer-seller commitment in new product development: (1) education and training of buyer and seller personnel, (2) training in mutual trust development, (3) co-location of personnel, (4) shared physical assets, and (5) formalized risk/reward sharing agreements. Taken together, this factor describes a level of involvement that simultaneously blends the two parties and defines the expectations and obligation of each through a formalized agreement.

Two questions that purchasing managers could use to assess commitment to a program of supplier involvement are:

1. Are the buyer and supplier sharing locations, physical assets, and personnel development?

2. Are there formalized risk/reward agreements between the buyer and supplier?

Answers of yes to both questions suggests a continuing commitment, an answer of no to one question suggests a limited commitment, and an answer of no to both questions suggests little commitment. While the answers to these questions are not definitive or prescriptive, they do provide insights that can help the purchasing manager focus his/her attention on the issue of buyer-supplier commitment.

Factor D-2: Explicit New Product Development Processes

This factor provides means of assessing the extent of formal processes that guide the selection and the extent of supplier involvement in new product development. Two items address the issue of supplier selection: the use of cross-functional teams and formal processes. Three items that focus on the extent of involvement are explicit supplier involvement in new product development teams, direct cross functional-communications between buyer and supplier personnel, and joint buyer-supplier agreements on new product development project performance measurements. Questions that purchasing managers can use to evaluate the extent of explicit new product development processes include:

1. Are cross-functional teams and formal processes used to select the suppliers to be involved in new product development?
2. Is the new product development program integrated with suppliers in terms of participation, communication, and establishment of performance measures when suppliers are involved?

Answers of yes to both these questions suggest the firm is actively managing the processes of selecting and involving suppliers in new product development. A no response to the first question suggests the buyer is (a) integrating suppliers into new product development projects but not actively managing the supplier selection process, or (b) managing suppliers that have been involved in new product development for a period of time. A no response to the second question suggests that the buyer is putting a lot of effort into selecting suppliers but not integrating them into the new product development process. A no response to both questions suggests supplier involvement in new product development is passively managed.

Factor D-3: Sharing Confidential Information

This factor addresses three issues relevant to the extent of information sharing between buyers and suppliers involved in new product development. A question purchasing management can ask about information sharing is: *Is information about technology and markets shared freely as necessary?* A yes response suggests suppliers have adequate information to be effectively involved in new product development. A no response suggests two further questions: *Is greater sharing of technical and customer information with suppliers needed?* and *Can our suppliers be adequately involved in new product development without sharing technical and market information?*

The following two factors address issues external to the involvement of purchasing and suppliers in the new product development process. These factors are included because the strategic orientation of the buyer and/or the forces of the external environment may affect strategy.

Factor E-1: Business Unit Competitive Responsiveness

Based on earlier research on time competitiveness, this factor assesses the respondent's perception of his/her business unit's performance. Two issues comprise this factor: The first is the ability of the organization to respond quickly to internal or external challenges. The second issue is the respondent's perception of their firm's strength as a competitor. This factor will be used in later analysis to evaluate the role of organizational strategy in (1) the involvement of purchasing and suppliers in new product development an (2) new product success.

Factor E-2: Competitive Hostility

Based on earlier research on the organization's external environment, this factor assesses the respondent's perception of the competitive environment faced by his/her organization. The perception of a competitive environment may create the sense of urgency and superordinate goals that motivate those in the organization to attempt challenges that otherwise might be disregarded. This factor will be used in later analysis to evaluate the role the organization's external environment plays in (1) the involvement of purchasing and suppliers in new product development, and (2) new product success.

NEW PRODUCT SUCCESS: INSIGHTS REGARDING PURCHASING AND SUPPLIER INVOLVEMENT

Issues That Affect New Product Success: Comparison of Mean Scores

A series of analyses were conducted to identify variables that affect new product success. The first step of this analysis was to divide the respondents to the new product development study into two categories (high and low) based on their scores on factor B-1: New Product Success. Respondent mean scores were compared using the t-test. Details of this analysis are presented in Appendix III. The results of the t-test revealed which factors were associated with the level of new product success.

As shown in Exhibit A-6, the mean scores of the following eight of 10 factors differed significantly between respondents who scored *high* on New Product Success and those who scored *low*:

B-1: Purchasing In a Major New Product Development Role
C-1: Strategic Evaluation and Control
C-3: Supplier Integration Outcomes
D-1: Continuing Commitment
D-2: Explicit Processes
D-3: Sharing Confidential Information
E-1: Business Unit Competitive Responsiveness
E-2: Competitive Hostility

Respondent factor scores of the following two factors did not differ significantly between respondents who scored *high* on new Product Success and those who scored *low*:

C-2: Suppliers in a Major New Product Development Role
C-5: Timing of Supplier Involvement

Respondents who consider their business units to be above average on product success are more likely to perceive that:

1. Purchasing plays a greater than average role in new product development. This includes becoming involved in new product development at the concept stage, playing an important role in cross-functional new product development teams, and playing an important role in identifying suppliers that offer competitive technology.

2. Supplier involvement in new product development is closely coordinated and controlled by the business unit. This includes evaluating whether new technology, new product time-to-market objectives, and quality objectives can best be achieved solely by the business unit or with a supplier. Finally, these business units work closely with suppliers to achieve target cost objectives.

3. Supplier integration into new product development processes results in reduced time-to-market and higher product quality.

4. There is a greater commitment to the buyer-supplier new product development relationship. This greater commitment includes shared education and training programs, co-location of supplier and business unit personnel, mutual trust training, shared physical assets, and formalized risk/reward sharing agreements.

5. A greater level of explicit agreement exists between the buyer and supplier regarding shared membership on new product development project teams; cross-functional, intercompany communications; and joint agreement on performance measures. In addition, the business unit is perceived as being more likely to use cross-functional teams for supplier selection and planning and more likely to have a formal process for selecting suppliers that will be integrated into the new product planning process.

6. They are more likely to share confidential business unit technical and customer information with suppliers.

7. Their business unit is a strong competitor; is more responsive to changing customer/supplier needs and competitor strategies; and more likely to develop and market new products better than competitors.

8. Their business unit is in a hostile market.

Perceptions of respondents who consider their business units to be above average on new product success were not significantly different from those of respondents who consider themselves below average, in the following areas:

1. The supplier's role in terms of importance, frequency of supplier use, or when the supplier becomes involved in the new product development process.

2. The timing of supplier involvement during the new product development process.

Apparently, the intensity or timing of supplier involvement do not significantly affect new product success, either positively or negatively.

Issues That Affect New Product Success: Regression Analysis

A second analysis was conducted to further evaluate the effects of the above variables on new product success. This analysis consisted of a regression analysis using Factor B-2: New Product Success as the dependent variable. One regression analysis was conducted with 156 of 168 respondents who indicated that suppliers are involved in new product development in their business units. A second regression analysis was conducted with 80 of 84 respondents who indicated that suppliers are not involved in new product development in their business units.

The subjects of the first regression analysis were respondents who indicated that suppliers are involved in new product development in their business units. The following eight independent variables used in this analysis were identified in the previous section as affecting new product success and were relevant to situations in which suppliers are involved in new product development:

B-1: Purchasing in a Major New Product Development Role
C-1: Strategic Evaluation and Control
C-3: Supplier Integration Outcomes
D-1: Continuing Commitment
D-2: Explicit Processes
D-3: Sharing Confidential Information
E-1: Business Unit Competitive Responsiveness
E-2: Competitive Hostility

As shown in Exhibit A-8, the following three independent variables entered the equation for respondents who involve suppliers in new product development:

B-1: Purchasing in a Major New Product Development Role
C-1: New Product Development Strategic Evaluation and Control
E-1: Business Unit Competitive Responsiveness

Factor C-1: Strategic Evaluation and Control explained 18.0 percent of the variance in New Product Success. The contributions of E-1: Business Unit Competitive Responsiveness, and B-1: Purchasing in a Major New Product Development Role to New Product Success variance were 6.5 percent and 3.0 percent respectively. The final equation was $(B\text{-}2) = 1.208 + 0.219(C\text{-}1) + 0.208(E\text{-}1) + 0.157(B\text{-}1)$ where scales for B-2, B-1, C-1, and E-1 are: 1 = Strongly Disagree to 5 = Strongly Agree. This equation explained 27.6 percent of the variance in New Product Success. The other 72.4 percent of the variance in New Product Success is explained by other variables such as product features, pricing decisions, promotional efforts, and distribution activities.

When suppliers are involved, the following three factors are likely to have an essential positive effect on new product success:

1. New Product Development Strategic Evaluation and Control (the careful evaluation of whether suppliers can contribute to technology/time-to-market/quality objectives, careful control of supplier integration into the new product development process, and close coordination of goals and efforts)
2. Business Unit Competitive Responsiveness (organizational commitment to time competitiveness)
3. Purchasing in a Major New Product Development Role (early purchasing participation, contributions to cross-functional teams, and proactive identification of those suppliers that can provide technological competitive advantages).

The subjects of the second regression analysis were respondents who indicated that suppliers are not involved in new product development in their business units. The following three independent variables used in this analysis were previously identified as affecting new product success and were relevant to situations in which suppliers are not involved in new product development:

B-1: Purchasing in a Major New Product Development Role
E-1: Business Unit Competitive Responsiveness
E-2: Competitive Hostility

As shown in Exhibit A-8, one variable entered the equation for respondents who do no involve suppliers in new product development. The variable, E-1: Business Unit Competitive Responsiveness, explained 35.8 percent of the variance in New Product Success. The final equation was $(B\text{-}2) = 1.355 + 0.487(E\text{-}1)$ where scales for B-2 and E-1 are: 1 = Strongly Disagree to 5 = Strongly Agree. This equation explained 35.8 percent of the variance in New Product Success. The other 64.2 percent of the variance in New Product Success is explained by other variables such as product features, pricing decisions, promotional efforts, and distribution activities.

When suppliers are *not* involved, one factor is likely to have an essential positive affect on new product success: Business Unit Competitive Responsiveness (organizational commitment to time competitiveness).

Issues That Affect Product Success: Overall Findings

One significant finding of the analysis of new product success is the role played by organizational strategy. The findings suggest that factor E-1: Business Unit Competitive Responsiveness is an essential condition for new product success. In the absence of a strong commitment by top management to organizational competitiveness, employee motivation to excel and the success of new products are likely to be reduced. This relationship is valid whether or not suppliers are involved in new product development.

A high level of Business Unit Competitive Responsiveness appears to help create the perception of a hostile competitive environment. The sense of urgency resulting from this perception may motivate purchasing to take a proactive role in new product development.

When suppliers are involved, two additional factors become essential to new product success: One factor is a blend of careful evaluation of whether or not to use suppliers, careful control of supplier integration into new product development, and close coordination of supplier efforts. The other factor is a purchasing department that can play a major role in new product development. This role includes early involvement, proactive participation in cross-functional teams, and the ability to identify those suppliers that can offer competitive advantage through technology.

The following other variables significantly affect new product success and may be catalyzed by organizational strategy, strategic evaluation and control, and purchasing's role:

D-1: Continuing Commitment
D-2: Explicit Processes
D-3: Sharing Confidential Information
E-2: Competitive Hostility

These findings indicate new product success is affected by an array of variables, some of which are controllable by purchasing and some of which are not. One uncontrollable variable, Business Unit Competitive Responsiveness, plays a significant role in new product success whether or not suppliers are involved. This result suggests purchasing managers should strive to play a proactive role in the organization's development of strategies that set the climate for successful new product development. In the absence of such a climate, any involvement by purchasing and suppliers will fail to produce a proportionate level of results.

In addition, two of eight controllable variables play significant roles when suppliers are involved in new product development. The development of strong purchasing capabilities in the areas of cross-functional team participation and proactive supplier identification combined with processes for effectively selecting, coordinating, and controlling suppliers can contribute positively to new product success.

Further, four of eight controllable variables affect new product success. However, the effectiveness of the following variables may be moderated by low levels of organizational competitive responsiveness, ineffective evaluation and control, and/or deficiencies in purchasing department capabilities:

C-3: Supplier Integration Outcomes
D-1: Continuing Commitment
D-2: Explicit Processes
D-3: Sharing Confidential Information

Finally, how extensively suppliers are involved (C-2: Suppliers in a Major New Product Development Role) and when they become involved (C-5: Timing of Supplier Involvement) do not appear to affect new product success. This finding is important to purchasing managers for two reasons:
1. *Purchasing is in a position to contribute to new product success whether or not suppliers are involved.* This means that purchasing departments that possess, or develop, the needed skills will be able to make positive contributions to new product success.
2. *The key to successful involvement of suppliers is the effective management of the supplier relationship.* This provides an excellent opportunity for purchasing, working as part of cross-functional, intercompany teams, to make positive contributions to new product success.

Supplier Involvement in New Product Development: Contributions to New Product Success

As shown in Exhibit A-7, respondents who include suppliers in the new product development process were compared to respondents who do not include suppliers in the new product development process. According to the t-test, the means of three out of four factors were significant at the 0.05 level. These significant factors were:

B-1: Purchasing in a Major New Product Development Role
B-2: New Product Success
E-2: Competitive Hostility

Respondent factor score means did not differ significantly at the 0.05 level on one factor:

E-1: Competitive Responsiveness

Respondents who include suppliers in the new product development process are more likely to perceive that:

1. Purchasing plays a greater role in new product development. This includes becoming involved in new product development at the concept stage, playing an important role in cross-functional new product development teams, and playing an important role in identifying those suppliers that offer competitive technology.

2. Business unit products are more successful in terms of meeting or exceeding sales objectives, profit objectives, and time-to-market schedule.

3. Their business unit is in a hostile market.

Perceptions of respondents who include suppliers in the new product development process did not differ from perceptions of those who do not use suppliers in the new product development process in the following area:

1. More likely to perceive their business unit as a very strong competitor by being more responsive to changing customer needs, supplier needs, and competitor strategies; more likely to develop and market new products better than competitors.

These results reveal that the respondents whose firms involve suppliers in new product development perceive new products, on average, to be more successful. This suggests purchasing managers should not lightly discard the idea of including suppliers in new product development programs. However, as stated in the previous section, the success of supplier involvement in new product development will be enhanced when purchasing can play an active role in new product development, suppliers are carefully selected and integrated into the new product development process, and the organization is an aggressive competitor.

OTHER VARIABLES AND PRODUCT SUCCESS

Respondents whose business units were owned by United States-based interests were more likely to perceive product success as high. One hundred twenty-two of 215 respondents (56.7%) whose business units were owned by U.S.-based interests perceived new product success as high. Ten of 19 respondents (52.6%) whose business units were not owned by U.S.-based interests perceived new product success as high. This difference was statistically significant at the 0.05 level. Any conclusion based on this finding should be guarded because of the small percentage (11.9%) of respondents whose business units were owned by other than U.S.-based interests.

Four variables were independent of perceived product success: industry category, business unit size, years experience in purchasing, and professional certification. Perceived product success did not differ among manufacturing, service, and other industry categories. Finally, years experience in purchasing or professional certifications did not vary with perceived product success. The finding that perceived new product success does not vary by industry category indicates the variables identified in this research are applicable to manufacturing and other industry categories.

OTHER VARIABLES AND SUPPLIER INVOLVEMENT IN NEW PRODUCT DEVELOPMENT

The following two variables were not independent of supplier participation in new product development: industry category and years experience in purchasing. Respondents in manufacturing were more likely to include suppliers in new product development. Respondents in services and other industries were less likely to include suppliers in new product development. This finding suggests there may be unrealized potential for supplier involvement in new product development in nonmanufacturing sectors of the economy.

While the data provided examples of high new product success and supplier involvement in nonmanufacturing, their relatively low occurrence suggests: (a) there are fewer opportunities for effective supplier involvement in new product development in nonmanufacturing firms, or (b) those in nonmanufacturing firms are less aware of the potentials for supplier involvement in new product development, or (c) nonmanufacturing firms have not capitalized on supplier involvement in new product development to the extent possible.

Purchasing managers in nonmanufacturing firms who do not involve suppliers in new product development should rethink that policy. The evidence from this research indicates that supplier involvement can contribute to new product success. Respondents who have more (11 or more years) experience in purchasing are more likely to include suppliers in new product development than are respondents with 10 or fewer years experience in purchasing. Apparently, more experienced purchasing managers are more aware of and better able to utilize suppliers in new product development projects.

THE RESEARCH ISSUES AND IMPLICATIONS FOR PURCHASING

The following sections summarize the findings concerning research issues identified early in this study. In addition, they summarize the implications of these findings for purchasing as well as the relationships among these research issues.

The Role of Purchasing

Purchasing plays a major role in new product development and in the management of supplier involvement in new product development. In new product development, purchasing plays three important roles: *First,* purchasing can contribute to new product success by becoming involved early in the new product development process. *Second,* purchasing can contribute to new product development by participating actively in cross-functional new product development teams. This participation will also include assuming a leadership role when appropriate. *Finally,* purchasing plays an important role in identifying high-potential suppliers.

According to the results, purchasing's role is essential to new product success when suppliers are involved. When suppliers are not involved in new product development, purchasing's role is significant, being associated with higher levels of new product success.

The implication is that purchasing must possess a wide range of capabilities if it is going to fulfill its potential contribution to new product development. These capabilities include, among others: (a) an overall awareness of the firm, its strategies, and objectives (b) a working knowledge of the technology and processes used in the firm's new product development process (c) good working relationships with other departments (d) strong interpersonal and leadership skills within the purchasing department (e) familiarity with existing suppliers (f) an awareness of the potentials of existing and prospective suppliers.

Supplier Identification/Certification

According to the research results, when suppliers are involved in new product development, careful evaluation of whether or not suppliers can contribute to technology/time-to-market/quality objectives, careful control of supplier integration, and close coordination of goals and efforts contribute directly to new product success.

The implication of this finding is that purchasing must be able to actively identify, screen, evaluate, and work with suppliers if it is to contribute effectively to new product success. The necessary capabilities are similar to those discussed in the previous section.

Close coordination and control of supplier participation in new product development suggests that supplier certification can play an important role in new product development. When supplier certification is sought, purchasing must have the necessary skills to coordinate the certification process and work effectively to implement the process internally and with suppliers.

Timing of Involvement

The results indicate that the exact timing of supplier involvement does not significantly affect new product success. As stated earlier, what is important is the ability to coordinate and control supplier efforts. Early supplier involvement, as such, does not appear to affect new product success. The optimum timing of supplier involvement is situational and is subject to coordination and control according to the buyer's needs.

This result indicates that one of the skills needed by purchasing is the ability to work effectively with cross-functional teams to (a) identify when suppliers should be included in new product development, (b) manage the supplier base so that qualified suppliers are available when needed, (c) effectively communicate team needs to suppliers, and (d) effectively communicate supplier needs to cross-functional teams.

Technology/Information Sharing

The results indicate that the regular sharing of technical, customer, product, and process information on an "as-needed" basis is associated with new product success. However, according to the regression analysis, its contribution is significant but not essential to product success.

A combination of Purchasing in a Major New Product Development Role and New Product Development Strategic Evaluation and Control are necessary to ensure that technology and information can be shared with confidence. The team skills required in the former and the close coordination required in the latter are necessary to provide the trust and control that enable sensitive information to be shared without fear of compromise.

Technology/information sharing means that purchasing must develop the confidence among suppliers and internal cross-functional team members to facilitate the candid sharing of needed information. In addition, purchasing must have the power to enforce ground rules for technology/information sharing, as well as the knowledge needed to serve as a bridge that can translate information among diverse participants.

Monitoring and Control

Effective monitoring and control contributes directly to product success when suppliers are involved in new product development. The following three components of monitoring and control were identified in factor C-1: New Product Development Strategic Evaluation and Control:

- the need to carefully evaluate whether a supplier can contribute to the new product project
- the need to effectively coordinate and control supplier involvement
- the need to work closely with suppliers to achieve objectives

To effectively monitor and control supplier involvement in new product development, purchasing must be able to participate meaningfully in decisions regarding whether or not to include suppliers in new product development. Also required is a high level of purchasing competence in supplier identification and qualification, supplier selection, negotiations, contributing to cross-functional teams, developing and administering multiparty agreements, and managing intercompany relationships.

Risk/Reward Sharing

Risk/reward sharing is included with shared education, training, personnel location, and assets in factor D-1: Continuing New Product Development Commitment. According to the regression analysis, its contribution is significant but not essential to product success.

Effective participation in risk/reward sharing by purchasing requires a good understanding of buyer and seller technologies; a grasp of development, start-up, and production costs from the perspectives of buyers and suppliers; the ability to create innovative contractual agreements that meet the needs of the buyer and supplier; an ability to anticipate contingencies; and a desire to seek agreements that are fair to all parties.

Time/Quality/Cost Savings

Time, quality, and cost considerations are included in factor C-1: New Product Development Strategic Evaluation and Control. According to the results of the analysis, these considerations (a) are best considered as part of the decision of whether or not to include suppliers in new product development, and (b) are issues essential to new product success when suppliers are involved.

To effectively participate in time/quality/cost savings issues, purchasing must be able to participate meaningfully in decisions regarding whether or not to include suppliers in new product development. As with monitoring and control, a high level of purchasing competence is needed in supplier identification and qualification, supplier selection, negotiations, and in contributing to cross-functional teams.

As with effective risk/reward sharing, purchasing's contributions to time/quality/cost savings require high levels of expertise in buyer and supplier technology; an understanding of development, start-up, and production costs from the perspectives of buyers and suppliers; the ability to create innovative contractual agreements that meet the needs of the buyer and supplier; an ability to anticipate contingencies; and a desire to seek agreements that are fair to all parties.

The Business Unit and Its Markets

According to the research results, Business Unit Competitiveness is essential to new product success whether or not suppliers are involved. The two issues in this factor, the business unit's ability to respond quickly to changes in the environment and its image as a strong competitor, provide cultural guidance that motivates those involved in new product development to succeed. Apparently, low levels of perceived competitive responsiveness reduce both the incentive of those in the organization and of involved suppliers to persevere in the challenge to develop successful products.

For purchasing managers and staff in competitive-oriented business units, the external motivation provided by the organization may provide the incentive to do well. However, the leadership of purchasing management will be needed to reinforce the organizational culture. When the business unit is not competitively orientated, the leadership of purchasing management can partially offset any motivational vacuum; however, the potential will be limited in such an environment.

The research results show that respondent perceptions of market competitive hostility are significant but not essential to product success. Apparently, the perception of the external threat helps create a superordinate goal that motivates those involved in new product development to strive to develop successful products.

Research Issues: Overall Findings

Careful examination of the results did not reveal significant findings beyond those discussed earlier. However, those findings can be restated in the context of the research issues as follows:

1. The business unit's competitive responsiveness is essential to new product success regardless of whether or not suppliers are involved in new product development.
2. Purchasing's role is essential to new product success when suppliers are involved in new product development, and important when suppliers are not.
3. Supplier identification and certification are important to new product success; however, careful evaluation of whether or not to use suppliers is essential to new product success when suppliers are involved.

4. The timing of supplier involvement in new product development is not associated with new product success.
5. Supplier monitoring and control are important but not essential to new product success.
6. Risk/reward sharing is important but not essential to new product success.
7. New product success in terms of sales, profits, time-to-market and quality are improved by supplier involvement in new product development.

CONCLUSIONS

Purchasing and Supplier Issues That Are Essential to New Product Success

This research identified three managerial variables essential to new product success: the business unit's orientation to time competitiveness, the thoroughness of the decision of whether or not to include suppliers in new product development, and purchasing's role in new product development.

1. Whether or not suppliers are involved in new product development, the organization's attitude toward time competitiveness will affect new product success. If suppliers are not involved in new product development, this is the only essential managerial variable identified in this study that contributes to product success.

2. If suppliers are involved in new product development, a combination of (a) careful evaluation of whether or not suppliers can contribute to new product objectives, and (b) close coordination and careful control of the efforts of selected suppliers are also essential to new product success.

3. If suppliers are involved in new product development, new product success will be enhanced if purchasing is in a major new product development role. This role includes early involvement in new product development, proactive participation in cross-functional teams, and active participation in identifying high-potential suppliers.

If suppliers are not involved in new product development, purchasing will be important but not essential to new product success. Apparently, the involvement of suppliers in new product development increases the importance of purchasing's ability to integrate the supplier with other functions in the business unit.

Our conclusion is that if these issues are not addressed effectively, other issues of purchasing and supplier involvement in new product development will not only fail to realize their full potential, but will also fail to compensate for lapses in the essential managerial variables.

Purchasing and Supplier Issues That Are Important but not Essential to New Product Success

This research also identified three managerial variables, one outcome, and one external environmental variable that are important to new product success:

1. The first managerial variable is *Continuing New Product Development Commitment.* This variable includes five components: (a) shared education and training, (b) shared plant and equipment, (c) co-location of buyer and supplier personnel, (d) formalized risk/reward sharing agreements, and (e) training in mutual trust development. Taken together, these five components create a framework for continuing cooperation.

2. The second managerial variable is *Explicit New Product Development Processes.* This variable focuses on the operational aspects of selecting and integrating suppliers into new product development programs. Two components of this managerial variable recognize the need to have formal processes for selecting suppliers once a decision has been made to involve suppliers in new product development. One component acknowledges the need for explicit agreements to establish the rules of involvement. The final two components formalize the interactive nature of supplier involvement in new product development.

3. The third managerial variable is *Sharing Confidential Information.* This frequent sharing of customer, product, and process technical information indicates the extent to which buyer and suppliers communicate when involved in new product development.

4. One outcome identified as being important to new product success is *Supplier Integration Outcomes.* The components of this outcome focus on new product time-to-market and quality. According to the results, supplier integration enhances time-to-market and product quality.

5. The environmental variable, *Competitive Market Hostility,* was associated with product success. Apparently, the perception of market competitiveness creates superordinate goals that provide the motivation to develop products that are successful.

6. The authors believe that these issues are most effective when the essential requirements for new product success are present. In their absence, the following issues will fail to achieve their potential.

Other Considerations

1. Purchasing and supplier involvement can have an impact on new product success in both manufacturing and service industry categories. Although the estimated response rate in non-manufacturing industry categories was lower, the effect of purchasing and supplier involvement in new product success did not differ from manufacturing respondents.

2. Neither purchasing nor supplier involvement in new product development were affected by country of ownership, respondent experience, or respondent professional certification.

STUDY B: PURCHASING AND SUPPLIER INVOLVEMENT IN PRODUCTION AND OPERATIONS PROCESS DEVELOPMENT AND IMPROVEMENT •

INTRODUCTION

Study A examined purchasing and supplier involvement in new product development with emphasis on the role played by suppliers. This study examines purchasing and supplier involvement in production/operations process improvement and development. In this study, process was defined *as any production/operations process that uses materials and supplies, capital equipment, labor, and information to convert inputs into products/services.* Process development/improvement was defined as *the procedures that guide the conceptualization, design, engineering, manufacturing, and implementation of changes to production/operations processes.*

Ten issues were addressed in the research purchasing and supplier involvement in new process development/improvement:

1. Supplier Involvement in Process Development/Improvement

2. Role of Purchasing

3. Supplier Identification/Certification

4. Timing of Involvement

5. Technology/Information Sharing

6. Monitoring and Control

7. Risks/Rewards

8. Time/Quality/Cost Savings

9. Importance of Process Development/Improvement Relative to New Product Development

10. The Business Unit and Its Markets

A detailed statistical analysis of responses to the questionnaire used to address these issues appears as Appendix IV. The following sections discuss the factors or concepts identified in this study and then relate these dimensions to the contributions of purchasing and suppliers to process development/improvement.

The following paragraphs are organized into seven sections. The first section discusses the factors resulting from the initial analysis of the data. These factors summarize the data into constructs that describe dimensions of purchasing and supplier involvement in production process development/improvement. The next section provides insights into production process as a source of competitive advantage. The next three sections discuss the involvement of purchasing, suppliers, and other variables in process development/improvement. The sixth section addresses the results relative to the research issues and discusses the implications of these results for purchasing. The final section presents the conclusions of Study B.

THE DIMENSIONS OF PURCHASING AND SUPPLIER INVOLVEMENT IN PRODUCTION PROCESS DEVELOPMENT/IMPROVEMENT

A statistical data reduction technique, called factor analysis, was used to simplify questionnaire responses and identify eight factors used to explain the involvement of purchasing and suppliers in new process development/improvement. Each factor, or concept, identified consists of two or more component statements that relate to the research issues. A description of these eight factors and their components follows, and the relationship between these factors and the research issues will be discussed.

Factor B-1: Process as a Source of Competitive Advantage

Five questionnaire items comprise this factor. They indicate that process contributes to competitive advantage (low cost, meaningful differentiation, or a combination of both) in the areas of cost, quality, and new product time-to-market. Further, process development/improvement is a high priority in the business unit for existing products.

An important implication for purchasing management is the need to focus on processes (how inputs are converted into outputs) as contributors to organizational objectives. Capabilities needed by purchasing in order to contribute to process development/improvement include (a) an understanding of the organization's processes, (b) knowledge of how processes can be improved, (c) an understanding of how processes contribute to competitive advantage, (d) an understanding of how purchasing can contribute to process development/improvement, and (e) an understanding of how suppliers can contribute to process development/improvement.

Five questions purchasing managers can ask to assess their understanding of process in their organization are:

1. Does purchasing understand the organization's processes?
2. Does purchasing understand how the organization's processes can be improved?
3. Does purchasing understand how processes contribute to competitive advantage in the organization, when competitive advantage refers to cost advantage, meaningful differentiation, or both?
4. Does purchasing understand how it can contribute to process development/improvement?
5. Does purchasing understand how suppliers can contribute to process development/improvement?

Answers of yes to all five questions suggest that purchasing is keenly aware of the role played by processes in the business unit. Answers of yes to most of the questions indicate that purchasing can improve its understanding of processes. Answers of no to most of these questions signify that purchasing is not in a position to contribute to process development/improvement.

Factor C-1:   Purchasing in a Major Process Development/Improvement Role

Purchasing must possess wide range of skills and abilities in order to play a major role in process development/improvement. These capabilities include (a) an overall awareness of the firm, its strategies, and objectives, (b) a working knowledge of process technology used to convert inputs into outputs, (c) good working relationships with other departments, (d) strong interpersonal and leadership skills within the purchasing department, (e) familiarity with existing suppliers, and (f) an awareness of the potentials of existing and prospective suppliers.

In order to evaluate purchasing's ability to play a major role in process development/improvement, an audit would be desirable. Six questionnaire items identified with the Purchasing in a Major Process Development/Improvement Role factor provide a basis for such an audit:

1. Does purchasing play a major role in process development/improvement?
2. Is purchasing constantly involved in process development/improvement?
3. Does purchasing play an important role in process development/improvement cross-functional teams?
4. Does purchasing take a leadership role in process development/improvement cross-functional teams?
5. Does purchasing play an important role in identifying technologies that are important to process development/improvement?
6. Does purchasing play an important role in identifying suppliers that are important to process development/improvement?

Answers of yes to these six questions indicate the purchasing department is positioned to contribute to process development/improvement. Answers of no to any of these questions suggest there is room for improvement in purchasing's capabilities. Further evaluation of the purchasing department's policies, management, and staff should identify specific areas for development.

Factor D-1:   Supplier Integration Process Development/Improvement Outcomes

This factor measures the outcome of supplier integration into process development/improvement. The four outcomes focus on reduced time-to-market, higher product quality, cost savings, and the achievement of cost objectives. The insights from this factor may be used by purchasing for post hoc analysis of supplier involvement in process development/improvement. Specific questions based on this factor would be:

1. Did supplier involvement reduce new product time-to-market?
2. Did supplier involvement result in higher new product quality?
3. Have cost savings resulted from process development/improvement shared with suppliers?
4. Do we work closely with suppliers to achieve cost objectives?

The answers to these questions might (a) lead to insights that improve suppliers' contributions to process development/improvement, (b) help evaluate whether continued supplier involvement can contribute to process development/improvement, or (c) determine whether cost saving potentials from process development are being realized. For example, answers of yes to the first three questions suggest that supplier involvement is contributing to organizational goals. A no response to any of these three questions suggests that an assessment of the goals, supplier contributions to these goals, or both would be warranted. Responses to question four can provide insights into the methods of working with suppliers.

Factor D-2: Openness to Supplier Involvement in Process Development/Improvement

This factor provides a means for assessing whether or not the business unit is open to supplier involvement in process development/improvement. While subjective in nature, the three questionnaire items that make up this factor provide a means of assessing the extent of the organization's openness to supplier involvement in process development/improvement. The combination of frequent use, close coordination, and receptiveness to supplier ideas define the concept as perceived by the research respondents.

This factor provides a means for purchasing managers to assess the extent to which suppliers are welcome to participate in process development/improvement. The following three questions can be used as a means of assessing how receptive the business unit is to supplier involvement:

1. Are suppliers used frequently for new product development?
2. Are supplier efforts closely coordinated with process development/improvement?
3. Are supplier ideas and recommendations welcome?

Answers of yes to these questions suggest the organization is receptive to supplier involvement in process development/improvement. Answers of yes to questions 1 and 2 and an answer of no to question 3 indicate that the potential of supplier involvement may not be fully realized. While every supplier suggestion is not going to be significant, negative attitudes may inhibit suppliers from presenting their ideas.

An answer of yes to question 3 and answers of no to questions 1 and 2 indicate that suppliers are involved in a minor role. This pattern of answers should raise the question: *Will greater supplier involvement contribute to process development/improvement?*

An answer of no to all three questions indicates minimal supplier involvement in process development/improvement. Two follow-up questions to these answers are: *Are there good reasons why suppliers are not involved in process development/improvement? and Are we missing opportunities by not involving suppliers in process development/improvement?*

In some cases more frequent and/or greater supplier involvement will improve process development/improvement. The point here is not that supplier involvement in process development/improvement is desirable for its own sake; rather, these questions should be asked and answered in the context of your business unit's needs.

Factor D-3: Process Development/Improvement Strategic Evaluation

This factor demonstrates the importance of careful evaluation of whether or not to involve a supplier in process development/improvement. Two components address this concern: (a) careful evaluation of whether new technology is better developed by the buyer or with a supplier, and (b) careful evaluation of whether process quality objectives can best be met by the buyer or with a supplier.

This factor raises two questions that purchasing management must consider:

1. Does purchasing have the skills and resources needed to contribute to the evaluation of whether process technology is best developed internally or with suppliers?
2. Does purchasing have the skills and resources needed to contribute to the evaluation of whether process quality objectives can best be developed internally or with suppliers?

Answers of yes to these questions suggest that purchasing is positioned to contribute to the evaluation of whether to use suppliers. Answers of no to either of these questions indicate that purchasing is not in a position to effectively contribute that decision process.

Factor D-5: Timing of Supplier Involvement in Process Development/Improvement

This factor provides a means of evaluating the timing of supplier involvement in process development/improvement. This factor helps to ascertain whether or not the actual timing of supplier involvement affects the success of process development/improvement programs.

The following two factors address issues external to the involvement of purchasing and suppliers in process development/improvement. These factors are included because the strategic orientation of the buyer and/or the forces of the external environment may affect strategy.

Factor E-1: Business Unit Competitive Responsiveness

Based on earlier research on time competitiveness, this factor assesses the respondent's perception of his/her organization. Two issues comprise this factor: The first is the ability of the organization to respond quickly to internal or external challenges. The second issue is the respondent's perception of their firm's strength as a competitor. This factor will be used in later analysis to evaluate the role of organizational strategy in the involvement of purchasing and suppliers in process development/improvement.

Factor E-2:   Competitive Hostility

Based on earlier research on the organization's external environment, this factor assesses the respondent's perception of the competitive environment faced by his/her organization. The perception of a competitive environment may create the sense of urgency and superordinate goals that motivate those in the organization to attempt challenges that otherwise might be disregarded. This factor will be used in later analysis to evaluate the role the organization's external environment plays in the involvement of purchasing and suppliers in process development/improvement.

PROCESS AS A SOURCE OF COMPETITIVE ADVANTAGE

Comparisons of Mean Scores

The first step in the analysis was to divide the respondents into two categories (high and low) based on their scores on factor B-1: Process as a Source of Competitive Advantage. Respondent mean scores were compared using the t-test. Details of the analysis are presented in Appendix IV. The results of the t-test revealed which factors were associated with process as a source of competitive advantage.

As shown in Exhibit B-6, the mean scores of the following six of seven factors differed significantly between respondents who scored *high* on Process as a Source of Competitive Advantage and those who scored *low:*

C-1: Purchasing in a Major Process Development/ Improvement Role
D-1: Supplier Integration in Process Development/ Improvement Outcomes
D-2: Openness to Supplier Involvement in Process Development/Improvement
D-3: Process Development/Improvement Strategic Evaluation
E-1: Business Unit Competitive Responsiveness
E-2: Competitive Hostility

Respondent factor scores for the following factor did not differ significantly at the 0.05 level:

Factor D-5:   Timing of Supplier Involvement in Process Development/Improvement

Respondents who consider their business units to be above average on process as a source of competitive advantage were more likely to perceive that:

1. Purchasing plays a major role in process improvement/development, including constant involvement, playing important roles in process improvement/development cross-functional teams, and in identifying technology and suppliers that are important to process development/improvement.

2. Supplier integration into process development/ improvement results in reduced product time-to-market and higher product quality; supplier identified cost savings are shared; and the business unit works closely with suppliers to achieve target cost objectives.

3. Supplier efforts are used frequently and are closely coordinated, and those responsible for process development/improvement are very receptive to supplier ideas.

4. Their business unit carefully evaluates whether new process technology and quality objectives are better met within the business unit or by suppliers.

5. Their business unit is a very strong competitor by being more responsive to changing customer needs, supplier needs, and competitor strategies.

6. Their business unit is a strong competitor in a hostile market.

Perceptions of respondents who consider their business units to be above average on process as a source of competitive advantage did not differ significantly from perceptions of those respondents who were below average in the following area:

1. Suppliers become involved in process improvement/development after the concept has been finalized.

Apparently, the timing of supplier involvement is not associated with the contribution of process development/improvement to competitive advantage.

Summary of Findings

The respondents perceive process development/improvement as a source of competitive advantage (low cost, meaningful differentiation, or both). The ability to improve the processes of converting inputs into outputs is important regardless of the freshness of the product line or the level of technology. Both purchasing and suppliers are perceived as being in a position to contribute to process development/improvement.

Purchasing managerial variables associated with process development/improvement include constant involvement, active participation in cross-functional teams, the identification of important technologies, and the identification of important suppliers. In addition, the careful evaluation of whether or not to use suppliers in process development/improvement is associated with the importance of process as a source of competitive advantage.

The management of suppliers is also important. Supplier integration into process development, close coordination, frequent use of suppliers, shared savings, and openness to supplier ideas are all associated with process as a source of competitive advantage.

Business unit competitive responsiveness and the perceived competitive hostility of the competitive environment were also perceived as associated with the importance of process to competitive advantage. The perception of a competitive environment that is hostile may contribute to the creation of superordinate goals that result in a strategy that is time competitive.

Overall, the development and improvement of production and operations processes is an issue of substantial importance where purchasing and supplier involvement can contribute to competitive advantage.

PURCHASING INVOLVEMENT IN PROCESS DEVELOPMENT/IMPROVEMENT

In this analysis the respondents were divided into two categories (yes and no) based on whether purchasing participates in process development/improvement in their business unit. Respondent mean scores were compared using the t-test on seven variables. As shown in Exhibit B-7, the mean scores of the following four variables were significant at the 0.05 level:

      B-1: Process as a Source of Competitive Advantage
      D-1: Supplier Integration in Process Development/ Improvement Outcomes
      D-2: Openness to Supplier Involvement in Process Development/Improvement
      D-5: Timing of Supplier Involvement in Process Development/Improvement

Three respondent mean scores that did not differ significantly at the 0.05 level involved the following variables:

      D-3: Process Improvement Strategic Evaluation
      E-1: Business Unit Competitive Responsiveness
      E-2: Competitive Hostility

Respondents whose business units' purchasing departments are involved in process development and improvement were more likely to perceive that:

1. Processes are a source of cost and quality advantage, contribute to product time-to-market schedules, and are high priority.

2. Supplier integration into process development/ improvement results in reduced product time-to-market and higher product quality; supplier identified cost savings are shared; and the business unit works closely with suppliers to achieve target cost objectives.

3. Supplier efforts are used frequently and are closely coordinated, and those responsible for process development/improvement are very receptive to supplier ideas.

4. Suppliers become involved in process improvement/development before the concept has been finalized.

Factor scores of respondents whose business units' purchasing departments are involved in process development did not differ at the 0.05 level from those who are not involved in the following areas:

1. Whether their business unit carefully evaluates whether new process technology and quality objectives are better met within the business unit or by suppliers.

2. Whether their business unit is a very strong competitor by being more responsive to changing customer needs, supplier needs, and competitor strategies.

3. Whether they perceive their business unit as being a strong competitor in a hostile market.

Summary of Findings

When purchasing participates in process development/ improvement, process is perceived as being more important to the business unit's sources of competitive advantage. Purchasing managers should be alert to the potential that process development/improvement offers and should be supportive of those who are interested in reviewing current operations/production processes for cost, quality, time responsiveness, and other benefits. As a minimum, the purchasing organization can contribute to the efforts of cross-functional teams, the identification of new technology, and the identification of potential new suppliers.

Purchasing is in an excellent position to facilitate the use of suppliers in process development programs by serving as a moderator, by helping suppliers to understand the process needs of the business unit, and helping those in other functions of the business unit appreciate the potentials and limitations of supplier involvement. Purchasing is also able to encourage supplier involvement in process development/improvement by promoting early, frequent, and closely coordinated participation. Overall, purchasing is well placed to facilitate the involvement of suppliers in process development/improvement activities. In many instances these activities will contribute to the business unit's competitive advantage.

SUPPLIER INVOLVEMENT IN PROCESS DEVELOPMENT/IMPROVEMENT

In this analysis the respondents were divided into two categories (yes and no) based on whether suppliers participate in process development/improvement in their business unit. As shown in Exhibit B-8, respondent mean factor scores were compared using the t-test. The following two variables were significant at the 0.05 level of statistical significance:

B-1: Process as a Source of Competitive Advantage
C-1: Purchasing in a Major Process Development/ Improvement Role

Respondent factor scores that did not differ significantly at the 0.05 level involved the following variables:

E-1: Business Unit Competitive Responsiveness
E-2: Competitive Hostility

Respondents whose business unit involved suppliers in process development and improvement are more likely to perceive that:

1. Processes are a source of cost and quality advantage, contribute to product time-to-market schedules, and are high priority.

2. Purchasing plays a major role in process improvement/development, is involved constantly, plays important roles in process improvement/development cross-functional teams, and identifies technology and suppliers that are important to process development/ improvement.

Factor scores of respondents whose suppliers are involved in process development did not differ at the 0.05 level from those whose suppliers were not involved, in the following areas:

1. Whether their business unit is a very strong competitor by being more responsive to changing customer needs, supplier needs, and competitor strategies.

2. Whether they perceive their business unit as being a strong competitor in a hostile market.

Summary of Findings

When suppliers are involved, purchasing is more likely to play a major role in process development/improvement. This means purchasing is well positioned to facilitate supplier involvement as discussed previously.

OTHER VARIABLES

Four other variables were analyzed to ascertain their effects on process as a source of competitive advantage, purchasing participation in process development/ improvement, and supplier participation in process development/improvement. These variables were industry category, nationality of business unit ownership, respondent experience in purchasing, and respondent certification (see Exhibit B-9).

The results indicated that nationality of business unit ownership, respondent experience in purchasing, and respondent certification did not have any affect on process as a source of competitive advantage or the participation of purchasing and suppliers in process development/improvement.

All three variables varied significantly with industry category. A higher percentage of respondents in manufacturing (61.9%) were categorized as "high" on Process as a Source of Competitive Advantage than respondents in the service (47.8%) or other (44.2%) industry categories. A higher percentage of respondents in service (95.7%) were categorized as "high" on Purchasing Participation in Process Development/Improvement than respondents in the manufacturing (84.0%) or service (69.1%) industry categories. Finally, a higher percentage of respondents in manufacturing (79.9%) were categorized as "high" on Supplier Participation in Process Development/Improvement than respondents in the service (68.1%) or other (65.5%) industry categories.

While process development/improvement varies among industry categories, these results indicate there is substantial interest and activity across industry categories. The implication for purchasing management and staff is that the potential of process development/ improvement should not be ignored in any industry category. Further, the potential for purchasing and supplier involvement should not be ignored in any industry category.

RESEARCH ISSUES AND IMPLICATIONS FOR PURCHASING

The following sections summarize the findings concerning the research issues identified earlier in this study as well as summarize the implications of these findings for purchasing. Finally, this section summarizes the relationships among these research issues.

Supplier Involvement in Process Development/ Improvement

Of 271 respondents, 203 (74.9%) indicated that suppliers participate in process development/ improvement. While supplier participation varied among industry categories, over 60 percent of respondents in each industry category (manufacturing, services, other) involve suppliers in process development/improvement.

The actual involvement of suppliers in process development/improvement is substantial. A comparison between supplier involvement in the two studies included in this report indicates that the level of supplier involvement in process development/improvement is comparable to the level of supplier involvement in new product development.

The implication for purchasing management is that the potential for purchasing and supplier contributions to process development/improvements is substantial. Purchasing skills in the areas of supplier and technology identification, supplier selection, mediating supplier and user needs and perspectives, and coordinating cross-functional needs are areas in which purchasing can facilitate the involvement of suppliers in process development/improvement.

Role of Purchasing

Purchasing plays significant roles in process development/improvement overall, and in the management of supplier involvement in process development/improvement. Purchasing can contribute by becoming involved early in process development/improvement programs, participating proactively in cross-functional teams, and by identifying high-potential technology and suppliers.

The implication is that purchasing must maintain a wide range of expertise if it is going to fulfill its potential contributions to process development/improvement. This potential includes (a) an awareness of the firm, its strategies, and objectives, (b) a working knowledge of the firm's technology and processes, (c) good working relationships with other departments, (d) strong interpersonal and leadership skills within purchasing, and (e) a working knowledge of existing and potential suppliers.

Supplier Identification and Certification

Careful evaluation of whether or not to use suppliers in process development/improvement projects does not appear to be of major concern to the respondents of this study. This may be due to the common use of suppliers in these projects. The identification of technology and suppliers appears to be more important than whether or not to use suppliers in process development/improvement.

The implication of this finding is that purchasing must be able to actively identify, screen, evaluate, and work with those suppliers that can contribute to process development/improvement programs.

Supplier certification can also play an important role in process development/improvement. This is especially important because of the common use of suppliers in these projects. When supplier certification is sought, purchasing must have the necessary skills to manage and coordinate the process with other functions and with suppliers.

Timing of Involvement

According to the research results, early involvement by purchasing contributes to process development/improvement; however, the timing of supplier involvement is not critical, overall. Apparently, the optimum timing of supplier involvement varies with the situation.

This result means that purchasing's skills should include the ability to work effectively with cross-functional teams to (a) identify when suppliers should be included in process development/improvement programs, (b) manage the supplier base so that technology and qualified suppliers are available when needed, (c) effectively communicate team needs to suppliers, and (d) effectively communicate supplier needs to other functions in the business unit.

Technology/Information Sharing

One questionnaire item addressed technology/information sharing. The mean score of that item (Suppliers are more likely to be integrated into Process Development/ Improvement when the project is technologically complex) was 3.69 on a scale of 1 (Strongly Disagree) to 5 (Strongly Agree). This item did not load on any interpretable factors. Statistical tests did not reveal any association of technology sharing with any other variables.

The research demonstrates that suppliers are more likely to be used in technologically complex process development/improvement projects. This means purchasing must develop an adequate level of technical ability to enable it to work effectively with suppliers and internal cross-functional team members. In addition, purchasing must develop the ability to translate information among the diverse participants in process development/improvement projects.

Monitoring and Control

Few questionnaire items loaded on interpretable factors. Those questions that did focused on coordination (see factors D-1 and D-3 in Exhibit B-4). Issues of supplier selection, commitment, and control did not enter into interpretable factors. This suggests that (a) little thought is given to supplier selection in process development/improvement projects, or (b) the technical nature of many process projects may limit the number of qualified suppliers, or (c) procedures for selecting suppliers for process projects are not well developed.

Risks/Rewards

Risk/reward sharing is included with supplier integration and cooperation in factor D-1: Supplier Integration in Process Development/Improvement Outcomes. This factor is associated with process as a source of competitive advantage and purchasing participation in process development/improvement.

Risk/reward sharing, as described in this study, requires that purchasing has a working knowledge of costs from the perspectives of the buyer and supplier, the ability to create innovative contracts that meet buyer and supplier needs, an ability to anticipate contingencies, and a desire to seek agreements that are fair to all parties.

Time/Quality/Cost Savings

Time, quality, and cost savings are integrated into factors B-1: Process as a Source of Competitive Advantage and D-1: Supplier Integration in Process Development/Improvement Outcomes. According to the results of the analysis, these considerations are included in the concepts of competitive advantage and supplier involvement outcomes.

To effectively contribute to time, quality, and cost savings in process development/improvement projects, purchasing must have high levels of proficiency in buyer and supplier technology, an understanding of process development/improvement processes, a working knowledge of the potentials and limitations of suppliers and their technology, and an ability to anticipate and manage contingencies.

Importance of Process Development/Improvement Relative to New Product Development

Because of the dearth of discussion of purchasing and supplier involvement in process development/improvement in the literature, respondent reaction to this study was greater than expected. The amount of supplier involvement in process development/improvement, and the distribution among industry categories, did not differ significantly from supplier involvement in new product development.

Evidently, both process development/improvement and new product development are important. The results of the two studies described in this report do not suggest that one is more important than the other. In addition, purchasing and suppliers can play important roles in both areas.

The results indicate that purchasing can contribute to both process development/improvement and new product development. Useful areas of purchasing expertise include (a) an overall understanding of the firm, its strategies, and objectives, (b) a working knowledge of process and new product technologies, (c) good working relationships with other departments, (d) strong interpersonal and leadership skills, (e) familiarity with existing and potential suppliers, (f) and the ability to coordinate multifunction programs with the business unit and suppliers.

The Business Unit and Its Markets

In process development/improvement, organizational time competitiveness and external environmental hostility affect the perceived importance of process as a source of competitive advantage. Their effects on whether or not purchasing and suppliers are involved in process development/improvement are not substantial. This may be due to the extensive involvement of purchasing and suppliers in process development/improvement in a wide range of situations.

Research Issues: Overall Findings

Careful examination of the results did not reveal significant findings beyond those stated previously. However, those findings can be restated in the context of the research issues as follows:

1. Production/operations process development and improvement is a source of competitive advantage (low cost, meaningful differentiation, or both) to business units in manufacturing, service, and other industry categories.
2. Purchasing plays an important role in process development/improvement whether or not suppliers are involved. This occurs in all industry categories.
3. Supplier involvement in process development/improvement is common in all three industry categories.
4. In process development/improvement, the identification of technology and suppliers is important. Because suppliers are frequently involved, the evaluation of whether or not to use suppliers in process development/improvement projects does not appear to be a vital concern.
5. The timing of supplier involvement in process development/improvement does not affect results. The best time to involve suppliers varies with the situation.
6. In supplier management, coordination is more important in process development/implementation than is supplier selection and control.

7. The importance of process development/ improvement to business unit competitive advantage is comparable to the importance of new product development.

8. While business unit competitive responsiveness and external environmental competitive hostility are associated with the perceived importance of process as a source of competitive advantage, they do not affect whether or not purchasing or suppliers are involved in process development/ improvement.

CONCLUSIONS

Process as a Source of Competitive Advantage

Process is an important source of competitive advantage (low cost, meaningful differentiation, or both). The level of importance is comparable to that of new product development. This conclusion does not imply any inherent conflict between these two priorities; however, emphasis on one priority at the expense of the other may be detrimental to overall business unit success. In many instances process development/improvement and new product development will occur simultaneously.

Purchasing management and staff must be aware of their potential for contribution to both process development/ improvement and new product development.

The Role of Purchasing in Process Development/ Improvement

Purchasing is often involved in process development/ improvement and often plays a major role. This role includes constant involvement, taking a proactive role in cross-functional teams, and actively seeking to identify technology that is important to process development/ improvement.

The Role of Supplier in Process Development/ Improvement

Suppliers are often involved in process development/ improvement and often play major roles. Supplier participation contributes to competitive advantage in the areas of new product time-to-market, higher quality, and cost savings.

Supplier Management in Process Development/ Improvement

Supplier management in process development/improvement focuses more on the identification of important technology and suppliers and on coordination rather than on supplier selection and control. This may be because process development/improvement for new and existing products is an ongoing process.

Industry Considerations

Process development/improvement offers the potential for competitive advantage in manufacturing, service, and other industry categories. Purchasing and supplier involvement in process development/improvement are substantial in all three industry categories.

Other Considerations

The study of purchasing and supplier involvement in process development/improvement warrants additional attention from academic researchers, practitioners, and the trade press.

SELF-CRITIQUE EXERCISES •

INTRODUCTION

This section provides the purchasing manager or executive with a means of applying the results of this research to his/her purchasing organization. Based on the research results, two self-critique exercises were developed. The first, A Self-Critique of Purchasing and Supplier Involvement in New Product Development, is designed to provide the user with insights into the roles of purchasing and suppliers in new product development. The second exercise, "A Self-critique of Purchasing and Supplier Involvement in Process Development and Improvement," is designed to provide the user with insights into the roles of purchasing and suppliers in the production/operations process development and improvement.

The insights from these exercises can be used in two ways: First, these exercises can be used as a starting point for self-evaluation. In this approach, the appropriate self-critique is used as a starting point to assess the roles of purchasing and suppliers in new product and/or process development. The insights from the critique can then be used to further evaluate the roles of purchasing and its suppliers.

A second approach would be to use these self-critiques after other self-critiques have been used as a means of verifying previously developed insights. In this approach, the self-critique exercise is used as a cross check on other evaluations.

As with any other organization evaluation technique, other evaluations should be used with these self-critiques as a means of verifying the results.

EXERCISE A: A SELF-CRITIQUE OF PURCHASING AND SUPPLIER INVOLVEMENT IN NEW PRODUCT DEVELOPMENT

Introduction

The purpose of this exercise is to provide managers with insights into the level of involvement of purchasing and suppliers in their business unit's new product development process. This exercise was developed as part of a research program funded by the Center for Advanced Purchasing Studies, Tempe, Arizona. While this exercise will provide useful managerial insights to those who complete and score the questions that appear in the exercise, the results of the exercise should not be considered as definitive or prescriptive.

Instructions

The exercise is comprised of four parts. Part A is a series of questions concerning your perception of your business unit regarding new product development and the role of purchasing and suppliers in the new product development process.

In Part B you score the results of your responses to Part A.

In Part C you chart the results of Part B.

In Part D you interpret and critique the results charted in Part C

When completing this exercise please keep in mind the following definitions:

BUSINESS UNIT refers to the company or division that you identify with in your job.

NEW PRODUCT refers to new products being marketed by your business unit to consumers, industrial customers, and or resellers.

NEW PRODUCT DEVELOPMENT PROCESS refers to the procedures that guide the conceptualization, design, engineering, production, and sourcing of a new product.

PART A. **PLEASE CIRCLE THE RESPONSE THAT BEST REFLECTS YOUR BUSINESS UNIT, USING THE FOLLOWING KEY:**

1 = STRONGLY DISAGREE   4 = AGREE
2 = DISAGREE   5 = STRONGLY AGREE
3 = NEITHER AGREE NOR DISAGREE

There are no "right" or "wrong" answers to any of these questions. What is needed is your frank and honest response. **DO NOT LOOK UP ANY INFORMATION IN YOUR BUSINESS UNIT'S RECORDS.** Only answers based on your perceptions and recollections are required.

	Strongly Disagree				Strongly Agree
1. In our Business Unit, the "typical" new product meets or exceeds its sales objectives	1	2	3	4	5
2. In our Business Unit, the "typical" new product meets or exceeds its profit objectives	1	2	3	4	5
3. In our Business Unit, the "typical" new product meets or beats its time-to-market schedule.	1	2	3	4	5
4. Purchasing plays a major role in the New Product Development Process.	1	2	3	4	5
5. Purchasing becomes involved in the New Product Development Process at the concept stage.	1	2	3	4	5
6. Purchasing plays an important role in New Product Development cross-functional teams.	1	2	3	4	5
7. Purchasing takes a leadership role in New Product Development cross-functional teams.	1	2	3	4	5
8. Purchasing plays an important role in identifying those suppliers that offertechnology that give our Business Unit competitive advantages.	1	2	3	4	5

Do suppliers participate in the New Product Development Process in your Business Unit? YES __ NO __ **IF "YES," GO TO QUESTION 9. IF "NO," GO TO PART B, "SCORING."**

	Strongly Disagree				Strongly Agree
9. Supplier efforts are closely coordinated with our Business Unit's New Product Development Process.	1	2	3	4	5
10. Supplier integration into the New Product Development Process is carefully controlled in our Business Unit.	1	2	3	4	5
11. Our Business Unit carefully evaluates whether new technology is better developed by ourselves or with a supplier.	1	2	3	4	5
12. Our Business Unit carefully evaluates whether new product time-to-market objectives can best be achieved by ourselves or with a supplier.	1	2	3	4	5
13. Our Business Unit carefully evaluates whether new product quality objectives can best be achieved by ourselves or with a supplier.	1	2	3	4	5

14. Our Business Unit works closely with suppliers to achieve target cost objectives during the New Product Development Process.

       1   2   3   4   5

15. Supplier integration into our New Product Development Process results in reduced time-to-market of new products.

       1   2   3   4   5

16. Supplier integration into our New Product Development Process results in higher product quality.

       1   2   3   4   5

Please circle the response that best describes the extent to which the following practices are used regarding supplier participation in your Business Unit's New Product Development Process using the following key:

1 = Never Used
2 = Almost Never Used
3 = Seldom Used
4 = Occasionally Used

5 = Used More Often Than Not
6 = Used In Most Situations
7 = Extensively Used

	Never Used						Extensively Used
17. Shared education and training programs between your Business Unit and suppliers.	1	2	3	4	5	6	7
18. Co-location of Business Unit and supplier personnel.	1	2	3	4	5	6	7
19. Training program in mutual trust development.	1	2	3	4	5	6	7
20. Shared physical assets (plant and equipment) between suppliers and your Business Unit.	1	2	3	4	5	6	7
21. Formalized risk/reward sharing agreements between your Business Unit and suppliers.	1	2	3	4	5	6	7
22. Supplier membership/participation on your Business Unit's New Product Development project team.	1	2	3	4	5	6	7
23. Direct cross-functional, intercompany communications between your Business Unit and suppliers.	1	2	3	4	5	6	7
24. Joint agreement on performance measurements of the New Product Development Process.	1	2	3	4	5	6	7
25. Business Unit cross-functional teams for supplier selection and planning.	1	2	3	4	5	6	7
26. Formal processes for selecting suppliers to be integrated into the New Product Development process.	1	2	3	4	5	6	7
27. Frequent technology information Sharing between your Business Unit and its suppliers on an "as-needed" basis.	1	2	3	4	5	6	7
28. Sharing customer requirements with suppliers.	1	2	3	4	5	6	7
29. Frequent and detailed sharing of product and process technology information between your Business Unit and its suppliers.	1	2	3	4	5	6	7

PART B.   SCORING

1. **New Product Success.** Add your responses for questions 1, 2, and 3. Enter the sum here____
    Divide the sum by 3. Enter that score here____

2. **Purchasing's Role in New Product Development.** Add your responses for questions 4 through 8. Enter the sum here____
    Divide the sum by 5. Enter that score here____

3. **New Product Development Strategic Evaluation and Control.** Add your responses for questions 9 through 14.
    Enter the sum here____
    Divide the sum by 6. Enter that score here____

4. **Outcomes of Supplier Integration in New Product Development.** Add your responses for questions 15 and 16.
    Enter the sum here____
    Divide the sum by 2. Enter that score here____

5. **Continuing New Product Development Commitment.** Add your responses for question 17 through 21. Enter the sum here____
    Divide the sum by 5. Enter that score here____

6. **Explicit New Product Development Processes.** Add your responses for questions 22 through 26. Enter the sum here____
    Divide the sum by 5. Enter that score here____

7. **Sharing Confidential Information.** Add your scores for question 27 through 29. Enter the sum here____
    Divide the sum by 3. Enter that score here____

PART C.   PLEASE CIRCLE THE NUMBER ON THE CONTINUUM THAT IS CLOSEST TO YOUR SCORE ON EACH OF THE SEVEN CATEGORIES.

	Standard Deviations		Mean	Standard Deviations	
	-2	-1	Mean	+1	+2
1. **New Product Success**	2.5	2.9	3.7	4.1	4.5
2. **Purchasing's Role in New Product Development**	1.9	2.8	3.7	4.6	5.01
3. **New Product Development Strategic Evaluation and Control**	2.8	3.3	3.8	4.3	4.8
4. **Outcomes of Supplier Integration in New Product Development**	2.7	3.3	3.9	4.5	5.0[1]
5. **Continuing New Product Development Commitment**	0.8	2.0	3.2	4.4	5.6
6. **Explicit New Product Development Processes**	2.2	3.3	4.4	5.5	6.6
7. **Sharing Confidential Information**	2.8	3.8	4.8	5.8	6.8

_____
[1]On this category, a value of 5.0 represents the maximum possible score rather than a true +2 standard deviation.

PART D.   INTERPRETATION AND DISCUSSION

The means and standard deviations represent the scores of purchasing executives who were categorized as "high" on new product success. For example, the value of 3.7 on New Product Success represents the mean score of purchasing executives who had been categorized into "high" on new product success. Similarly, the value of 4.1 on New Product Success represents the mean score of purchasing executives who were one standard deviation above the mean, or in the 84th percentile of purchasing executives who had been categorized into "high" on New Product Success. A value of 2.9 on New Product Success represents the mean score of purchasing executives who were one standard deviation below the mean, or the 16th percentile. Finally, values of 4.5, two standard deviations above the mean, and 2.5, two standard deviations below the mean, would be in the 98th and 2nd percentiles respectively.

1.   Interpretation of Results

   a.   Category scores that are near the mean value indicate that your perception of your business unit's situation is comparable to the average of those respondents whose New Product Success score is "high."
   b.   Values near "positive" standard deviations indicate that your perception of your business unit's situation is above average compared to those respondents whose New Product Success score is "high."
   c.   Values near "negative" standard deviations indicate that your perception of your business unit's situation is below average compared to those respondents whose New Product Success score is "high."

Respondents whose business unit's suppliers do not participate in new product development will be able to complete categories 1 and 2 (New Product Success and Purchasing's Role in New Product Development).

Connecting the circled values should give you a visual picture of your business unit's perceived performance compared to business units that scored "high" on New Product Success.

To examine a category more closely, you may want to examine your response to individual questions in that category. For example, assume your score for category 2 (Purchasing's Role in New Product Development) was 2.8, well below average compared to those respondents whose New Product Success was "high." Further assume that your responses to items 4 through 8 were 3, 3, 2, 2, and 4 respectively. Inspection of these items suggests that you perceive purchasing as not playing a significant role in cross-functional teams. This could mean that your business unit does not form cross-functional teams, or that purchasing is not active in existing cross-functional teams. In the former situation, you might want to explore the usefulness of cross-functional teams in your business unit. In the latter situation, you might want to increase purchasing's effectiveness in your business unit's cross-functional teams.

2.   Critique

In the space provided write a brief critique of each category as it applies to your business unit. Include positive and negative comments, overall assessment, areas for improvement, and one or two suggestions for improvement.

1.   **New Product Success**
   a.   Positive and Negative Comments _____
   b.   Overall Assessment _____
   c.   Areas for Improvement _____
   d.   Suggestions for Improvement _____

2.   **Purchasing's Role in New Product Development**
   a.   Positive and Negative Comments _____
   b.   Overall Assessment _____
   c.   Areas for Improvement _____
   d.   Suggestions for Improvement _____

3.   **New Product Development Strategic Evaluation and Control**
   a.   Positive and Negative Comments _____
   b.   Overall Assessment _____
   c.   Areas for Improvement _____
   d.   Suggestions for Improvement _____

4. **Outcomes of Supplier Integration in New Product Development**
   a. Positive and Negative Comments _____
   b. Overall Assessment _____
   c. Areas for Improvement _____
   d. Suggestions for Improvement _____

5. **Continuing New Product Development Commitment**
   a. Positive and Negative Comments _____
   b. Overall Assessment _____
   c. Areas for Improvement _____
   d. Suggestions for Improvement _____

6. **Explicit New Product Development Processes**
   a. Positive and Negative Comments _____
   b. Overall Assessment _____
   c. Areas for Improvement _____
   d. Suggestions for Improvement _____

7. **Sharing Confidential Information**
   a. Positive and Negative Comments _____
   b. Overall Assessment _____
   c. Areas for Improvement _____
   d. Suggestions for Improvement _____

8. Please record a brief summary of the results of your analysis below:

   _____
   _____

   _____
   _____

   _____
   _____
   _____

EXERCISE B: A SELF-CRITIQUE OF PURCHASING AND SUPPLIER INVOLVEMENT IN PRODUCTION AND OPERATIONS PROCESS DEVELOPMENT AND IMPROVEMENT

Introduction

The purpose of this exercise is to provide managers with insights into the level of involvement of purchasing and suppliers in their business unit's process development/improvement. This exercise was developed as part of a research program funded by the Center for Advanced Purchasing Studies, Tempe, Arizona. While this exercise will provide useful managerial insights to those who complete and score the questions that appear in the exercise, the results of the exercise should not be considered as definitive or prescriptive.

Instructions

The exercise is comprised of four parts. Part A is a series of questions concerning your perception of your business unit regarding process development/improvement and the role of purchasing and suppliers in process development/improvement.

In Part B you score the results of your responses to Part A.

In Part C you chart the results of Part B.

In Part D you interpret and critique the results charted in Part C

When completing this exercise please keep in mind the following definitions:

46

BUSINESS UNIT refers to the company or division that you identify with in your job.

PROCESS refers to any production/operations process that uses materials and supplies, capital equipment, labor, and information to convert inputs into products/services.

PROCESS DEVELOPMENT/IMPROVEMENT refers to procedures that guide the conceptualization, design, engineering, manufacturing, and implementation of changes to production/operations processes.

PART A. PLEASE CIRCLE THE RESPONSE THAT BEST REFLECTS YOUR BUSINESS UNIT, USING THE FOLLOWING KEY:

1 = STRONGLY DISAGREE	**4 = AGREE**
2 = DISAGREE	**5 = STRONGLY AGREE**
3 = NEITHER AGREE NOR DISAGREE	

There are no "right" or "wrong" answers to any of these questions. What is needed is your frank and honest response. **DO NOT LOOK UP ANY INFORMATION IN YOUR BUSINESS UNIT'S RECORDS.** Only answers based on your perceptions and recollections are required.

	Strongly Disagree				Strongly Agree
1. In my Business Unit processes are a source of cost advantage.	1	2	3	4	5
2. In my Business Unit processes are a source of quality advantage.	1	2	3	4	5
3. The processes of my Business Unit contribute to meeting or beating new product time-to-market schedules.	1	2	3	4	5
4. Process Development/Improvement is a high priority in my Business Unit.	1	2	3	4	5
5. Process Development/Improvement is a high priority in my Business Unit for existing products.	1	2	3	4	5

Does purchasing participate in process development/improvement in your business unit? YES___ NO___ IF YES, GO TO QUESTION 6. IF NO, GO TO THE STATEMENT FOLLOWING QUESTION 11.

	Strongly Disagree				Strongly Agree
6. Purchasing plays a major role in Process Development/Improvement.	1	2	3	4	5
7. Purchasing is constantly involved in Process Development/Improvement.	1	2	3	4	5
8. Purchasing plays an important role in Process Development/Improvement cross-functional teams.	1	2	3	4	5
9. Purchasing takes a leadership role in Process Development/Improvement cross-functional teams.	1	2	3	4	5
10. Purchasing plays an important role in identifying technology that is important to Process Development/Improvement.	1	2	3	4	5
11. Purchasing plays an important role in identifying suppliers that are important to Process Development/Improvement.	1	2	3	4	5

Do suppliers participate in process development/improvement in your business unit? YES___ NO___ IF YES, GO TO QUESTION 12. IF NO, GO TO PART B: SCORING.

	Strongly Disagree				Strongly Agree
12. Supplier integration into Process Development/ Improvement results in reduced-time-to market of new products.	1	2	3	4	5
13. Supplier integration into Process Development/ Improvement results in higher product quality in my Business Unit.	1	2	3	4	5
14. Suppliers share in the cost savings they identify in Process Development/Improvement projects.	1	2	3	4	5
15. My Business Unit works closely with suppliers to achieve target cost objectives during Process Development/Improvement projects.	1	2	3	4	5
16. Suppliers are frequently involved in Process Development/Improvement.	1	2	3	4	5
17. Supplier efforts are closely coordinated with Process Development/Improvement in my Business Unit.	1	2	3	4	5
18. Those responsible for Process Development/ Improvement in my Business Unit are very receptive to ideas that come from our suppliers.	1	2	3	4	5
19. Our Business Unit carefully evaluates whether new process technology is better developed by ourselves or with a supplier.	1	2	3	4	5
20. Our Business Unit carefully evaluates whether process quality objectives are better met by ourselves or with a supplier.	1	2	3	4	5

PART B.   SCORING

1. **Process as a Source of Competitive Advantage.** Add your responses for questions 1 through 5. Enter the sum here
    Divide the sum by 5. Enter that score here___

2. **Purchasing in a Major Process Development/Improvement Role.** Add your responses for questions 6 through 11. Enter the sum here___
    Divide the sum by 6. Enter that score here___

3. **Supplier Integration in Process Development/Improvement Outcomes.** Add your responses for questions 12 through 15. Enter the sum here___
    Divide the sum by 4. Enter that score here___

4. **Openness to Supplier Involvement in Process Development/ Improvement.** Add your responses for questions 16 through 18. Enter the sum here___
    Divide the sum by 3. Enter that score here___

5. **Process Development/Improvement Strategic Evaluation.** Add your responses for questions 19 and 20. Enter the sum here___
    Divide the sum by 2. Enter that score here___

PART C. PLEASE CIRCLE THE NUMBER ON THE CONTINUUM THAT IS CLOSEST TO YOUR SCORE ON EACH OF THE FIVE CATEGORIES.

	Standard Deviations		Mean	Standard Deviations	
	-2	-1		+1	+2
1. **Process as a Source of Competitive Advantage**	3.8	4.1	4.4	4.7	5.02
2. **Purchasing in a Major Process Development/ Improvement Role**	2.5	3.2	3.9	4.6	5.0[1]
3. **Supplier Integration inProcess Development/ Improvement Outcomes**	2.6	3.2	3.8	4.4	5.0
4. **Openness to Supplier Involvement in Process Development/Improvement Projects**	2.6	3.2	3.8	4.4	5.0
5. **Process Development/Improvement Strategic Evaluation**	2.0	2.8	3.6	4.4	5.0[1]

PART D. INTERPRETATION AND DISCUSSION

The means and standard deviations represent the scores of purchasing executives who were categorized as "high" on Process as a Source of Competitive Advantage. For example, the value of 4.4 on Process as a Source of Competitive Advantage represents the mean score of purchasing executives who had been categorized into "high" on Process as a Source of Competitive Advantage. Similarly, the value of 4.7 on Process as a Source of Competitive Advantage represents the mean score of purchasing executives who were one standard deviation above the mean, or in the 84th percentile of all respondents. A value of 4.1 on Process as a Source of Competitive Advantage represents the mean score of purchasing executives who were one standard deviation below the mean, or in the 16th percentile of all respondents. Finally, values of 3.8, two standard deviations below the mean, and 5.0, two standard deviations above the mean, would be in the 2nd and 98th percentiles respectively.

1. Interpretation of Results

   a. Category scores that are near the mean value indicate that your perception of your business unit's situation is comparable to the average of those respondents whose Process as a Source of Competitive Advantage score is "high."
   b. Values near "positive" standard deviations indicate that your perception of your business unit's situation is above average of those respondents whose Process as a Source of Competitive Advantage score is "high."
   c. Values near "negative" standard deviations indicate that your perception of your business unit's situation is below the average of those respondents whose Process as a Source of Competitive Advantage score is "high."

Respondents whose business unit's suppliers do not participate in new product development will be able to complete categories 1 and 2 (Process as a Source of Competitive Advantage and Purchasing in a Major Process Development/ Improvement Role).

Connecting the circled values should give you a visual picture of your business unit's perceived performance compared to business units that scored "high" on Process as a Source of Competitive Advantage.

To examine a category more closely, you may want to examine your response to individual questions in that category. For example, assume your score for category 2 (Purchasing in a Major Process Development/Improvement Role) was 3.0, well below average compared to those respondents whose Process as a Source of Competitive Advantage "high." Further assume that your responses to items 6 through 11 were 3, 3, 2, 2, 4, and 4 respectively. Inspection of these

---

[1]On this category, a value of 5.0 represents the maximum possible score rather than a true +2 standard deviation.

items suggests that you perceive purchasing as not playing a significant role in cross-functional teams. This could mean that your business unit does not form cross-functional teams, or that purchasing is not active in existing cross-functional teams. In the former situation, you might want to explore the usefulness of cross-functional teams in your business unit. In the latter situation, you might want to increase purchasing's effectiveness in your business unit's cross-functional teams.

2. Critique

In the space provided write a brief critique of each category as it applies to your business unit. Include positive and negative comments, overall assessment, areas for improvement, and one or two suggestions for improvement.

1. **Process as a Source of Competitive Advantage**
   a. Positive and Negative Comments _____
   b. Overall Assessment _____
   c. Areas for Improvement _____
   d. Suggestions for Improvement _____

2. **Purchasing in a Major Process Development/Improvement Role**
   a. Positive and Negative Comments _____
   b. Overall Assessment _____
   c. Areas for Improvement _____
   d. Suggestions for Improvement _____

3. **Supplier Integration in Process Development/Improvement Outcomes**
   a. Positive and Negative Comments _____
   b. Overall Assessment _____
   c. Areas for Improvement _____
   d. Suggestions for Improvement _____

4. **Openness to Supplier Involvement in Process Development/ Improvement Projects**
   a. Positive and Negative Comments _____
   b. Overall Assessment _____
   c. Areas for Improvement _____
   d. Suggestions for Improvement _____

5. **Process Development/Improvement Strategic Evaluation**
   a. Positive and Negative Comments _____
   b. Overall Assessment _____
   c. Areas for Improvement
   d. Suggestions for Improvement

6. Please record a brief summary of the results of your analysis below:

_____
_____

_____
_____

_____
_____
_____

APPENDIX I: ANNOTATED BIBLIOGRAPHY •

This bibliography is divided into three sections. The first section includes sources that were important in our study of the new product development topic. The second section includes sources that we found important to the new product development topic. The final section includes sources that were important to the process development/improvement topic.

I. SOURCES IMPORTANT TO NEW PRODUCT DEVELOPMENT

A. Akacum and B.G. Dale, "Supplier Partnering: Case Study Experiences," *International Journal of Purchasing and Materials Management,* Vol. 31 No. 1 (Winter 1995), pp.38-44.

This article describes the findings of partnership sourcing practices of 11 firms in Manchester, United Kingdom. Key aspects of partnering examined were integrated design, open-book accounting, and the sharing of risks and benefits. Generally, partnering was established for: (1) high-volume purchase items and products of strategic importance to the firm, (2) specialized products that require information and training for effective use, (3) services that require an understanding of the process, and (4) no previous supplier could meet material requirements (p. 39).

Personal relationships and mutual trust, rather than contracts, were the driving forces of the partnerships. While price was a key factor, common characteristics of the partnerships included training, quality assurance audits, regular meetings to monitor accomplishments, joint problem solving, quality improvement, and operational-level information exchange. Open-book policies, sharing of savings resulting from value engineering, and joint proactive quality improvement procedures were practiced by only two companies. All firms were prepared to upgrade operations and develop capabilities to meet customers' unique requirements (p. 41). *This suggests that supplier involvement in NPD might also be looked at from the suppliers' perspectives.*

Two firms had high levels of cooperation with their suppliers (pp. 42-43). Emphasis seems to be on the developments of long-term relationships through supplier certification. While NPD was not explicitly mentioned, process development seems to be a continuation of the overall ongoing relationship. The benefits and limitations of partnering are discussed (p. 43).

Cooperative relationships seem to be formed for materials and services that have strategic importance. Further, personal relationships were considered to be more important than contracts in making partnerships work. Partnerships existed between single customer-supplier pairs. There was no interaction among suppliers.

Ian Barclay, "The New Product Development Process: Past Evidence and Future Practical Application, Part 1," *R&D Management,* Vol. 22, No.3 (July 1992), pp.255-263.

This article reviewed the NPD literature over the last four decades and synthesized five attributes found to be of importance to new product success:
1. an open minded, supportive, and professional management
2. a good market knowledge and strategy
3. a unique and superior product
4. good communications and coordination
5. proficiency in technological activities

Ian Barclay, "The New Product Development Process: Part 2. Improving the Process of New Product Development," *R&D Management,* Vol. 22, No.4 (October 1992), pp.307-317.

The article reviews NPD process models proposed by past research, reviews NPD processes found within 149 companies, and describes a structured evaluation and improvement methodology. Attempts at practical modeling include the Booz, Allen, and Hamilton model widely used in marketing textbooks and other models (p. 308). Quantification of NPD success is described (p. 310), and change processes of the NPD process are described (p. 311+). The experiment described in the article was inconclusive. There is no mention of supplier involvement.

Richard Beltramini, "Concurrent Engineering: Information Acquisition Between High Technology Marketeers and R & D Engineers in New Product Development," *International Journal of Technology Management,* Vol. 11, Nos. 1&2 (1996), pp. 58-69.

This article empirically assesses the informational interface between research and development engineers and marketing in high-technology companies. An interdisciplinary team of academics from several universities developed a benchmark survey instrument. This article reports on a nationwide survey of 481 high-technology U.S. durable goods manufacturers. Five factors accounted for the majority of variance (Table 1, p. 63): Organizational Structure, Informational Characteristics, Timing, Training, and Resources. Results parallel earlier cited research.

This article provides good model for questionnaire development and a reference list of articles relating to communication among functional groups.

Laura M. Birou and Stanley E. Fawcett, "Supplier Involvement in Integrated Product Development: A Comparison of U.S. and European Practices," *International Journal of Physical Distribution and Logistics Management,* Vol. 24, No. 5 (1994), pp. 4-14.

The authors use an empirical study to compare U.S. and European practices in NPD and Integrated Product Development (IPD). The authors conclude that U.S. respondents have moved further than European respondents. Intense competition, especially from foreign competitors, may have stimulated U.S. firms to be more active in supplier involvement. The authors conclude that competitive imperatives may create opportunity to instigate organizational and interorganizational change (p. 13). Purchasing managers must develop working relationships with manufacturing, marketing, and R&D (p. 13).

Five specific facilitating roles purchasing can play (pages 13-14) include: (1) cataloguing suppliers' technical and design expertise, (2) promoting earlier supplier involvement, (3) building stronger buyer-supplier relationships, (4) developing a "committed" environment that will enable suppliers to be more creative and risk-acceptant, and (5) facilitating better and more consistent communication (pp. 13-14).

Andrea Bonaccorsi and Andrea Lipparini, "Strategic Partnerships in New Product Development: An Italian Case Study," *The Journal of Product Innovation Management,* Vol. 11, No. 2 (March 1994), pp.134-145.

This article address the NPD process, partnering with suppliers, use of teams, time competitiveness, and target costs. Pages 136 and 137 provide an excellent presentation of partnering models. Pages 136+ focus on the benefits from partnering at the NPD level. Pages 142+ describe the product process as it cuts across functions at the product development stages (concept development, product planning, engineering, production, and launch and support).

Robert G. Cooper and Elko J. Kleinschmidt, "An Investigation into the New Product Process: Steps, Deficiencies, and Impact," *The Journal of Product Innovation Management,* Vol. 3, No. 2 (June 1986), pp. 71-85.

The authors found that what firms do is miles apart from what the literature prescribes (see focus on 13 new product activities, Exhibit 1, p. 74). Impact on Success (p. 80) indicates that (a) three activities strongly related to project outcomes were: initial screening, preliminary technical assessment, and product development and (b) six activities significantly related to project outcomes were: preliminary market assessment, market research/detailed market study, business/financial analysis, in-house product tests, test market/trial sell, and market launch. Further analysis indicated that the following seven activities stood out as particularly key: initial screening, preliminary market assessment, detailed market study/market research, business/financial analysis, product development, in-house product tests, and market launch. According to Table 13 (p. 84), three critical activities often overlooked or weakly handled were: detailed market study/market research, initial screening, and preliminary market assessment. Implications (pp. 84-85) include the need for a new product process model; a need for discipline; more time, effort, and resources; and more focus on key activities.

Robert G. Cooper, "The Components of Risk in New Product Development: Project NewProd," *R&D Management,* Vol. 11, No.2 (1987), pp. 47-54.

This article focuses on risk in NPD and includes a good literature review on risk. Four rules of thumb for managers/firms seeking to avoid or minimize NPD risk were: seek projects that are synergistic within the firm, avoid projects new to the firm, beware of projects that involve high technology (big ticket items), and stay clear of dynamic markets. Finally, it was concluded that managers appraise risk more in terms of the amounts at stake than in the uncertainties of the situation.

Jeffrey H. Dyer, "How Chrysler Created an American Keiretsu," *Harvard Business Review,* Vol. 74, No. 4 (July-August 1996), pp.42-56.

This article reviews the evolution of Chrysler's product development-supplier relationship process. Much of the impetus for change came from Chrysler's financial crisis of the 1980s and its acquisition of American Motors Corporation (AMC). The financial crisis provided the motivation, and the experience of AMC in working with its suppliers provided the initial model.

Chrysler's new model (pp. 50-56) features (1) cross-functional teams, (2) presourcing and target costing, (3) total value-chain improvement, (4) enhanced communication and coordination, and (5) long-term commitments. This article provides an in-depth review of the evolution of early supplier involvement in new product development at Chrysler.

The author emphasized the importance of top management commitment, using initial successes to further the change effort, and the importance of listening to suppliers as components of total supplier involvement. The trial-and-error nature of this change process was also mentioned.

Abbie Griffin, "Evaluating QFD's Use in U.S. Firms as a Process for Developing Products," *The Journal of Product Innovation Management,* Vol. 9, No. 3 (September 1992), pp. 171-187.

The author addresses the Quality Functional Deployment (QFD) as a response to the shortcomings of the phase-review process approach to product development (Table 1, p. 174). QFD produced little measurable short-term improvement but did result in significant intangible benefits (pp. 178-180).

Suggestions for improving NPD processes in general included (1) structure decision-making across functional groups, (2) build a solidly organized, highly motivated team, and (3) move information efficiently from its origin to the ultimate user. Overall, QFD may have benefits subject to its limitations.

Abbie Griffin, "Metrics for Measuring Product Development Cycle Time," *The Journal of Product Innovation Management,* Vol. 10, No. 2 (March 1993), pp. 112-125.

This article presents a method for obtaining NPD cycle-time baselines. Professor Griffin reviews the literature and observes that previous research on NPD cycle times suffers from: (1) a lack of rigor, (2) comparing apples to oranges - is the product developed from scratch or is the new product incrementally changed from a previous product, and what time frames are measured - how are conception, production, and first sales defined? (pp. 113-114)

The research reported focuses on project characteristics, process development variables, and measures of process and product outcomes (pp. 115-120). Findings suggest that product development time was affected by: (1) percent change across product generations, (2) product complexity, and (3) whether or not a formal process was used. Suggestions for future research are included.

Necmi Karagozoglu and Warren B. Brown, "Time-Based Management of the New Product Development Process," *The Journal of Product Innovation Management,* Vol. 10, No. 3 (June 1993), pp.204-215.

In a study of 31 West Coast high-technology firms, 77 percent, developed new products based on expansions of existing technology, 23 percent of the firms performed fundamental research on new technology, 52 percent attempted to lead competition based on incremental advances in existing technology, 35 percent competed on new products embodying new technology (including externally developed technology), 13 percent competed by introducing improvements in product price and performance, 45 percent occasionally used external sources of technology, and 23 percent extensively used external sources of technology.

Extent of use of multifunctional teams, and problems with their use, are discussed on pages 209 and 210. A higher percentage of firms (61%) used multifunctional teams in downstream phases than in predevelopmental phases (31%). The authors presume that time-based management of NPD develops idiosyncratic solutions, rather than generalized approaches. It appears that a barrier to accelerating NPD processes may be adherence to the status quo.

Douglas W. LaBahn, Abdul Ali, and Robert Krapfel, "New Product Development Cycle Time: The Influence of Project and Process Success Factors in Small Manufacturing Companies," *Journal of Business Research,* Vol. 36, No. 2 (June 1996), pp. 179-188.

The authors examined NPD cycle time in small manufacturing companies. Table 4 (p. 185) indicates the following independent variables affect NPD cycle time: Project size, technical content, and non-technical outside assistance. The relationship between output control and NPD cycle time was found to be dependent on the extent of product innovation and expected short-term market growth rate. Product innovation and output control by themselves were not significant in the regression model.

Jordan D. Lewis, *The Connected Corporation* (New York: The Free Press, 1995) ISBN 0-02-919055-X.

This book addresses a wide range of issues regarding working with suppliers in a variety of situations. The author provides excellent insights regarding most aspects of multi-firm alliances. This book is essential for anyone working with multifirm alliances.

Vincent A. Mabert, John F. Muth, and Roger W. Schmenner, "Collapsing New Product Development Times: Six Case Studies," *The Journal of Product*

Innovation Management, Vol. 9, Vol. 3 (September 1992), pp. 200-212.

The article reviews traditional serial and concurrent NPD and identifies four issues that affect NPD time: motivation, the workings of teams, outside cooperation with teams (including suppliers, the model shop, customers, and others), and project control. Table 2 (p. 211) details specific suggestions in each of four issues.

Eduardo G. Mendez and John N. Pearson, "Purchasing's Role in Product Development: The Case for Time-Based Strategies," *International Journal of Purchasing and Materials Management,* Vol. 30, No. 1 (January 1994), pp. 3-12.

The authors suggest that purchasing can play a more active role in the new product development process through its participation in a cooperative multi-disciplinary team approach. Page 4 includes a table comparing traditional and time-based companies. Page 6 includes a table presenting changes in purchasing responsibilities between 1980 and 1988. Figure 3 on page 9 presents a time-based NPD team structure; however, this team structure has each team member responsible for isolated issues. There seems to be little collaboration among the team members for these issues. Figure 4 on page 10 suggests a purchasing organization that facilitates time-based product development strategies.

Kentaro Nobeoka and Michael A. Cusumano, "Multiproject Strategy, Design Transfer, and Project Performance: A Survey of Automobile Development Projects in the U.S. and Japan," *IEEE Transactions on Engineering Management,* Vol. 42, No. 4 (November 1995), pp. 397-409.

The authors explore the relationship between different multiproject strategies and project performance. The article includes a good literature review (p. 397), a framework of multiproject strategies (p. 398), and a model of types of design transfer (pp. 399-400). Five issues affect rapid interproject design transfer (pp. 403-405): (1) advance planning, (2) mutual adjustments, task sharing, and joint design, (3) transfer of "fresh" versus "dated" design, (4) problems of "anonymous" design, and (5) the role of a general manager for multiproject management. Issues of communication between project managers, organizational structure, and strategic/organizational consideration are also addressed.

The key conclusion is the rapid design transfer among multiple projects using overlapping coordination.

Gary L. Ragatz, Robert B. Handfield, and Thomas V. Scannell, "Success Factors for Integrating Suppliers Into New Product Development," *The Journal of Product Innovation Management,* Vol. 14, No. 3 (May 1997), pp. 190-202.

The authors examined companies' most and least successful supplier integration efforts based on (1) management practices employed and (2) NPD project environment.

Twelve management practices were significantly different between most and least successful NPD projects (p. 10): (1) supplier participation, (2) direct cross-functional communication, (3) shared education and training, (4) common and linked information systems, (5) co-location of buyer/seller personnel, (6) technology sharing, (7) formal trust development processes/practices, (8) customer requirements information sharing, (9) technology information sharing, (10) shared physical assets - plant and equipment, (11) formalized risk/reward sharing agreements, and (12) joint agreement on performance measures.

Four NPD project environmental factors were significantly different between most and least successful NPD projects (p. 11): (1) familiarity with supplier's capabilities prior to integration in this project, (2) strength of supplying firm top management commitment to their involvement, (3) strength of consensus that right supplier was selected, and (4) strength of buying firm top commitment to supplier integration.

Ernest Raia, "Teaming in Detroit," *Purchasing,* Vol. 116, No. 3 (March 3, 1994), pp. 40+.

The article mentions greater systems responsibility being given to "Tier One" suppliers, and also includes and excellent discussion of Chrysler's teaming approaches on page 45.

Hirotaka Takeuchi and Ikujiro Nonaka, "The New Product Development Game," *Harvard Business Review,* Vol. 64, No. 1 (January-February 1986), pp. 137-146.

This article presents a holistic approach to new product development. Six characteristics of this approach are: built-in instability, self-organizing project teams, overlapping development phases, multilearning, subtle control, and organizational transfer learning. Exhibit II on page 139 provides a comparison of sequential product development and two types of overlapping product development. Limitations and managerial implications of this holistic approach are discussed.

Ravi Venkatesan, "Strategic Sourcing: To Make or Not to Make," *Harvard Business Review,* No. 70, No.6 (November-December 1992), pp.98-107.

The author addresses the issue of making survival sourcing decisions of highly engineered products based on three principles: (1) focus on components that are critical to the product and that the company is distinctively good at making, (2) outsource components for which suppliers have a distinct competitive advantage, and (3) use outsourcing as a means of generating employee commitment to improving manufacturing performance.

According to the article, sourcing decisions are often the result of confused thinking about (1) comparative advantage, (2) supplier management, and (3) economies of scale. This confused thinking is due to: conflicting priorities due to poor coordination, feeling that suppliers are opportunistic, the difficulty of assigning opportunity costs to misdirected management and engineering talent, and a fear that outsourcing would reduce the ability of the firm to differentiate its products (pp. 99-100).

Subsystems should be classified as strategic when they: (1) have high impact on important product attributes, (2) require skills and assets that are not available from independent suppliers, and (3) involve technology that is fluid and where there is a significant likelihood of gaining a clear technological lead (pp. 101-102). For strategic subsystems, two more questions that need to be answered are: (1) what are the relative suppliers' design and manufacturing capabilities and (2) is the cost of catching up to the best suppliers affordable to the company?

Architectural knowledge (the ability to capture customer requirements and translate them into subsystem performance specifications), not manufacturing capabilities as such, is the key to competitiveness (p. 102). By remaining expert on architectural knowledge the ability to control the design and manufacture of the subsystem becomes more important than actually producing the subsystem. The article addresses the processes of deciding whether to make-or-buy.

Billie Jo Zirger and Modesto A. Maidique, "A Model of Product Development: An Empirical Test," *Management Science,* Vol. 36, No.7 (July 1990), pp. 867-883.

This five year study examined over 330 new products in the electronics industry. The authors found from an extensive literature search that new products were likely to be successful when (quoted from p.871):

1. The firm had an in-depth understanding of its customers and the marketplace.
2. The firms markets proficiently and commits a significant amount of its resources to selling and promoting successful products.
3. The firm's R&D is efficiently planned and well executed.
4. The firm's R&D, production, and marketing functions are well coordinated.
5. The firm provides a high level of management support for the product from the development stage through its launch to the marketplace.
6. The product has a high performance to cost ratio.
7. The product benefits significantly from the firm's existing market and technology strengths.
8. The product provides a high contribution margin to the firm.
9. The market has few competing products.

The article provides a good model of the critical elements of product development (p. 872) but no indication where suppliers fit in.

A factor analysis of the empirical data identified eight factors (p. 877): (1) R&D Excellence, (2) Marketing and Manufacturing Competence, (3) Synergy with Existing Competencies, (4) Superior Technical Performance, (5) Large and Growing Market, (6) General Management Support, (7) Weak competitive Environment, and (8) Product Value. All eight factors were significant at the <0.05 level in the multiple discriminate model, which accurately correctly predicted success or failure in 88 percent of the original samples.

II. SOURCES IMPORTANT TO NEW PRODUCT DEVELOPMENT

Paul S. Adler, Avi Mandelbaum, Vien Nguyn, and Elizabeth Schwerer, "From Project to Process Management: An Empirically-based Framework for Analyzing Product Development Time," *Management Science,* Vol. 41, No. 3 (March 1995), pp. 458-484.

The authors conclude that their results encourage further research. Technical impediments (p. 482) to process modeling are (1) the lack of order in product design, (2) the complexity of process modeling, and (3) product development often occurs as streams of development rather than as discrete activities. Organizational Impediments (pp. 482-483) include: (1) engineering managers focus on unique features of each project, (2) engineering managers lack requisite data, and (3) engineers tend to be "autonomous" professionals who are reluctant to develop process models.

Paul S. Adler, Avi Mandelbaum, Vien Nguyn, Elizabeth Schwerer, and Elizabeth Schwerer, "Getting the Most Out of Your Product Development Process," *Harvard Business Review*, Vol. 74, No. 2 (March-April 1996), pp. 134-152.

> This article advocates the application of process management to product development. The authors found that the product development process benefits from (1) projects get done faster if the organization does fewer projects at a time, (2) investments that relieve bottlenecks yield disproportionate time-to-market benefits, and (3) eliminating unnecessary variations in workloads and work processes frees up the organization to focus on creative parts of the process. A comprehensive example illustrates the lessons discussed earlier. No insights into supplier involvement in the product development process are provided.

David N. Burt and William R. Soukup, "Purchasing's Role in New Product Development," *Harvard Business Review*, Vol. 63, No. 5 (September-October 1985), pp. 90-97.

> By forging links between purchasing and engineering, the authors argue that an enhanced role of purchasing in NPD can help incorporate suppliers into design processes. Specific recommendations for connecting purchasing with engineering include (1) colocation, (2) multifunction reviews, (3) project teams, (4) recommended parts lists, (5) procurement engineers, and (6) employee rotation.

James Carbone, "Chrysler Tries the Partnering Role," *Electronic Business Buyer*, Vol. 19, No. 11 (November 1993), pp. 97-99.

> This article focuses on Chrysler's program of partnering with suppliers and getting them involved early in the new product development process. According to the article, Chrysler engineers work closely with suppliers during the design stage and tap their technical brainpower. According to Louise Linder, director of electrical and electronic procurement at Chrysler, supplier early involvement was essential in keeping the price and development time of the Omni down to about $10,000 and 31 months. Purchasers, engineers, and quality engineers are on commodity teams and manage suppliers. With the Neon and LH, Chrysler chose suppliers immediately after the design state, but before the design stage. Suppliers had to commit to target costs. "Open book" pricing is used to manage costs without eroding supplier margins. Chrysler's goals include quality, delivery, and EDI. Chrysler is moving toward becoming a virtual company in which you will not be able to tell the difference between Chrysler and a

supplier in the NPD process. Suppliers will be an extension of Chrysler. The authors consider this one of the best trade journal articles on the subject.

James Carbone, "Purchasing Gets Into the Product-Development Act," *Electronic Business Buyer*, Vol. 20, No. 4 (May 1994), p. 75.

> 74 percent of the respondents to an Electronic Business Buyer survey said that purchasing is more involved in NPD than it was five years ago. 79 percent of the buyers surveyed said that semiconductor and electromechanical suppliers are involved in NPD at the concept or design stage. Suppliers are involved to lower the cost of the product as early as possible.

Robert G. Cooper, "A Process Model for Industrial New Product Development," *IEEE Transactions on Engineering Management*, Vol. EM-30. No.1 (February 1983), pp. 2-11.

> Synthesis of the NPD literature resulted in the following six lessons regarding NPD (pp. 4-6):
> 1. for industrial products, a much stronger market orientation is needed,
> 2. new product success is largely amenable to management action,
> 3. there is no easy explanation for what makes a new product a success,
> 4. the product itself — a unique product real customer advantages — is central to success,
> 5. a well-conceived, properly executed launch is vital to success, and
> 6. internal communication and coordination between internal groups greatly fosters successful innovation.
>
> A seven stage industrial NPD process model is presented.

Michael A. Cusumano, "Manufacturing Innovation: Lessons from the Japanese Auto Industry," *Sloan Management Review*, Vol. 30, No. 1 (Fall 1988), pp. 29-39.

> Japanese automakers pursued three basic policies (pp. 32-34): JIT manufacturing, temporary reduction of process complexity, and vertical "de-integration." Vertical "de-integration" involved building up networks of subsidiaries and other subcontractors while decreasing the levels of in-house vertical integration between component production and final assembly. The authors infer from this article that supplier involvement in NPD by the Japanese automakers may be more a result of policies regarding vertical de-integration. American firms, in my opinion, may be pursuing supplier involvement independent of any vertical integration, or vertical de-integration, policy.

Michael A. Cusumano and Akira Takeish, "Supplier Relations and Management: A Survey of Japanese, Japanese-Transplant, and U.S. Auto Plants," *Strategic Management Journal,* Vol. 12, No. 8 (1991), pp. 563-588.

A 1990 empirical study indicates that: (1) Japanese firms rely on fewer parts suppliers and have closer relations with these suppliers, (2) Japanese suppliers have their own suppliers while American firms tend to buy lower-level components (p. 564), (3) Japanese automakers tend to select their suppliers at the product-development stage and rate them by value while American firms select suppliers annually through competitive bidding, (4) Japanese suppliers become more involved earlier and to a greater extent than U.S. suppliers (p. 565), (5) American firms rely on market forces while Japanese firms emphasize target prices, (6) Japanese suppliers provide higher quality, and (7) there is much more information exchange among Japanese firms and their suppliers (see Table 1, p. 567, for summary of issues).

Table 16 on page 577 summarizes the results. The implication is that there are differences between U.S. and Japanese supplier relations and management practices (pp. 582-584). While U.S. automakers and suppliers have become more effective, the Japanese appeared to meet these challenges aggressively. Japanese transplants resembled their parent-firms in most areas of management style and performance. These transplant firms were making excellent progress in supplier development (p. 583). Further, there has been a large-scale movement of Japanese suppliers to the United States. Finally, the authors touch on the strategic benefit of buying from U.S. suppliers.

David L. Deeds and Charles W.L. Hill, "Strategic Alliances and the Rate of New Product Development: An Empirical Study of Biotechnology Firms," *Journal of Business Venturing,* Vol. 11, No. 1 (January, 1996), pp.41-55.

The authors studied 132 biotechnology firms in the United States. It was found that a firm's rate of NPD is initially a positive function of the number of strategic alliances. However, this relationship exhibits diminishing, and then negative, returns if a firm enters into too many strategic alliances.

"Design Case Histories: A Look At Purchasing's Role in Forging the Design Link," *Purchasing,* Vol. 97, No. 5 (September 6, 1984), pp. 88-104.

This article provides several short case histories regarding successful supplier participation NPD/ product improvements.

Anne Donnellon, "Cross-functional Teams in Product Development: Accommodating the Structure to the Process," *The Journal of Product Innovation Management,* Vol. 10, No. 5 (November 1993), pp.377-392.

This article concludes that a challenge to cross-functional teams in NPD is that team work provides numerous paradoxes and contradictions for individuals, teams, and organizations (p. 392).

Shad Dowlatshahi, "Purchasing's Role in a Concurrent Engineering Environment," *International Journal of Purchasing and Materials Management,* Vol. 28, No. 1 (Winter 1992), pp. 21-25.

This article examines purchasing involvement in product design and development. Purchasing is more effective when it is an integral part of a concurrent engineering environment. Purchasing's role in concurrent engineering include (1) development of specifications, (2) parts interchangability, (3) parts standardization and simplification, (4) value analysis, (5) part substitutions, (6) part exclusions, and (7) miscellaneous contributions. The author concludes that purchasing's role must be tailored to each company. No mention is made of supplier involvement in this article.

Somerby Dowst, "Better-Forged Links Bring in Better Designs," *Purchasing,* Vol. 97, No. 5 (September 6, 1984), pp. 67-75.

This article presents a good comparison of the following issues between 1980 and 1994: (1) how often purchasing gets advance notice of design plans, (2) where purchasing gets its notice, (3) how often purchasing calls on suppliers for design aid, and (4) how suppliers apply their expertise. Compared to 1980, in 1984 (1) purchasing gets earlier notice of design plans, (2) purchasing is more likely to sit on committees with marketing or engineering and provide cost estimates on new projects, (3) purchasing is slightly more likely to call suppliers for design aid, and (4) suppliers are slightly more likely to apply their expertise in tolerances, standardization, order sizes, process changes, packaging, and inventory; slightly less likely to apply their expertise in material specifications and transportation; and neither more or less likely to apply their expertise to buyer plant assembly changes.

Scott J. Edgett, "The New Product Development Process for Commercial Financial Services," *Industrial Marketing Management,* Vol 25, No. 6 (1996), pp. 507-515.

This article focuses on new product development success factors in the financial services industry.

Findings include: (1) a rigorous new product process is important to success, (2) early up front marketing activity is essential, (3) quality of execution is a must, and (4) success is manageable. The roles of purchasing and suppliers are not discussed in this article.

John E. Ettlie, "Product-Process Development Integration in Manufacturing," *Management Science,* Vol. 41, No. 7 (July 1995), pp. 1224-1237.

This literature review indicates that (1) firms that successfully introduce new products are focused and better able to understand their customers' needs and (2) successful product innovators are more disciplined in their development process (p. 1224); however, it is the authors' opinion that the data, results, and conclusions do not make much sense.

David Farmer, "The Role of Procurement in New Product Development," *International Journal of Physical Distribution and Materials Management,* Vol. 11, Nos. 2/3 (1981), pp.46-54.

This article argues that there is a place for procurement in product development.

Susan Helper, "How Much Has Really Changed Between U.S. Automakers and Their Supplier?" *Sloan Management Review,* Vol. 32, No. 4 (Summer 1991), pp. 15-28.

Figure 1 (p. 16) provides a supplier-relations matrix based on information exchange and commitment. Pre-1980 supplier relations in the U.S. auto industry were "exit" based (low on both commitment and information exchange). This author concludes that supplier relations in this industry are at a crossroad — suppliers feel that information sharing has increased but trust has not (p. 24). Relations are a compromise between exit and voice. A possible outcome is "tiering" in which only a few "first-tier" suppliers deal directly with the customer, assuming responsibility for procurement of parts for the system. Authors' comment: tiering buffers second and third level suppliers from dealing with the customer and simplifies transactions.

Richard T. Hise, Larry O'Neal, James U. McNeal, and A. Parasuraman, "The Effect of Product Design Activities on Commercial Success Levels of New Industrial Products," *The Journal of Product Innovation Management,* Vol. 6, No. 1 (March 1989), pp. 43-50.

The authors surveyed 195 manufacturers of industrial products. The authors found that when the cumulative number of product design activities increased (i.e., rough drawings, detailed drawings, crude working models, testing crude working models, prototype designs, testing prototype performance, and final modifications), higher product success rates were achieved. It was concluded that the technical aspects of product design should be carefully considered as companies seek ways to improve commercial performance of new industrial product offerings.

Richard T. Hise, Larry O'Neal, A. Parasuraman, and James U. McNeal, "Marketing/R&D Interaction in New Product Development: Implications for New Product Success Rates," *The Journal of Product Innovation Management,* Vol. 7, No. 2 (June 1990), pp.142-155.

The authors studied the product development practices of 252 U.S. firms. The authors found that greater levels of marketing involvement per se do not increase the success of new consumer and industrial products (p. 154). However, when marketing and R&D demonstrate high levels of joint efforts in product final design, new consumer and industrial products are likely to have higher levels of success. Further, the authors found that marketing/R&D cooperation should focus on the day-to-day, "nitty-gritty" aspects of physically shaping the product.

G. David Hughes and Don C. Chafin, "Turning New Product Development into a Continuous Learning Process," *The Journal of Product Innovation Management,* Vol. 13, No. 2 (March 1996), pp. 89-104.

The Value Proposition Process consists of four iterative loops addressing capturing market value, adding business value, delivering a winning solution, and applying project and process planning. According to the authors, the process encourages flexibility, makes cross-functional interaction and communication easier, and helps transform the organization to become a market driven organization and externally focused. The roles of purchasing and suppliers are addressed in this article.

Fahri Karakaya and Bulent Kobu, "New Product Development Processes: An Investigation of Success and Failure in High-Technology and Non-High-Technology Firms," *Journal of Business Venturing,* Vol. 9, No.1 (January 1994), pp.49-66.

The authors present a thorough review of the literature on product success and failure. New product failure was grouped into two major categories, NPD process and environmental factors (pp. 60-62).

Edward F. McDonough, III and Raymond M. Kinnunen, "Management Control of New Product Development Projects," *IEEE Transactions on Engineering Management,* Vol. EM-31, No.1 (February 1984), pp. 18-21.

The authors studied seven successful and five unsuccessful projects. "Successful" was defined as a project which met or exceeded sales and profit/ROI expectations (p. 19). Four insights regarding NPD control systems were identified (pp. 19-20):

1. Setting goals for new product projects - cost budgets and schedules were set for all projects; however, problems in setting goals were compounded by unfamiliarity with the technology and/or market, pressure on the project leader by marketing and sales, and looser initial product specifications (and the later in the project they became defined) increased the likelihood of product failure.

2. Three devices were used to monitor projects — written reports, formal meetings, and informal meetings. Real control was found to be best exercised by close informal supervision.

3. Management response to deviations is an area requiring greater attention. Management usually felt limited in the responses they could take.

4. Incentives for performance were the weakest aspect of control systems observed. Management did not tie individual rewards to NPD budget, goals, or commercial success.

Edward F. McDonough III and Gloria Barczak, "Speeding Up New Product Development: The Effects of Leadership Style and Source of New Technology," *The Journal of Product Innovation Management,* Vol. 8, No. 3 (September 1991), pp 203-211.

Based on a study of 30 NPD projects in 12 British firms, the authors found that (a) a participatory leadership style facilitates NPD speed of development when the technology is developed internally and (b) leadership style (participatory vs. nonparticipatory) does not greatly affect NPD speed of development when the technology is acquired from external sources (pp. 208-209).

Rudy K. Moenaert and William E. Souder, "An Information Transfer Model for Integrating Marketing and R&D Personnel in New Product Development Projects, *The Journal of Product Innovation Management,* Vol. 7, No. 2 (June 1990), pp. 91-107.

The authors developed a model for processing information between marketing and R&D during NPD.

Robert M. Monczka, Ernest L. Nicols, Jr., and Thomas J. Callahan, "Value of Supplier Information in the Decision Process," *International Journal of Purchasing and Materials Management,* Vol. 28, No. 2 (Spring 1992), pp. 20-30.

This article studies types of information that purchasing professionals use in making sourcing decisions, the value they attach to different types of information, and identify the perceived value of different types of information relative to the type of purchase, size of the buying firm, and the individual's position level. Purchase categories were (1) raw materials, (2) engineered products - unique, (3) engineered products - standard, (4) MRO, (5) capital equipment, and (6) construction. Construction was not included in the analysis because there were only three respondents.

Fourty-four variables (N = 103) were factor analyzed, and 12 factors were identified (p. 25): (1) supplier capabilities, (2) financial position and potential threats, (3) supplier size, (4) socioeconomic information, (5) distribution network, (6) pricing, (7) price/volume history, (8) performance ratings, (9) advanced supplier capabilities, (10) delivery information, (11) customer/industry served, and (12) payment terms.

Customer ratings of supplier quality performance, customer ratings of supplier delivery performance, and total lead-time by commodity ranked among the five most valuable supplier information types for all purchase categories. Past price paid and engineering support/design service capability ranked among the eight most valuable supplier information types for all purchase categories.

It was concluded that buyers of different commodities and materials place different values on different types of supplier information used to make purchasing decisions (see pp. 28-29 for specifics).

Eric M. Olson, Orville C. Walker, Jr. and Robert W. Ruekert, "Organizing for Effective New Product Development: The Moderating Role of Product Innovativeness," *Journal of Marketing,* Vol. 59, No. 1 (January 1995), pp. 48-62.

The authors question whether cross-functional teams are a universal panacea for shortening development times and improving success rates in all types of NPD projects. The data supports the contingency model which suggests that (a) cross-functional teams are more likely to improve NPD effectiveness and timeliness when the product being developed is truly new and innovative and (b) bureaucratic structures produce better outcomes on less innovative products, such as line extensions or product improvements.

Charles O'Neal, "Concurrent Engineering with Early Supplier Involvement: A Cross-Functional Challenge," *International Journal of Purchasing and Materials Management,* Vol. 29, No. 2 (Spring 1993), pp. 3-9.

The author looks at customer value in terms of CV = Q/C + R, where CV is customer value, Q are those quality attributes perceived to be important to the customer, C is total cost of ownership, and R is the customers' perception of responsiveness over time as the customers' needs and expectations change over time. The impact of concurrent engineering (CE) and early supplier involvement (ESI) on cycle-time reduction is discussed. According to the author, the most significant features of CE are customer focus and cycle-time reduction. This results in higher quality, reduced cost, and reduced cycle time. Effective CE requires early, sustained involvement by key materials suppliers. The author concludes that CE and ESI offer great promise.

William D. Presutti, Jr., "Technology Management: An Important Element in the Supplier Capability Survey," *International Journal of Purchasing and Materials Management,* Vol. 27, No. 1 (Winter 1991), pp. 11-15.

The author conducted a survey of 146 Pittsburgh area firms. The composition of supplier on-site evaluation teams and the activities evaluated by these teams is reported.

Joyce Ranney and Mark Deck, "Making Teams Work: Lessons from the Leadership in New Product Development," *Planning Review,* Vol. 23, No. 4 (July/August 1995), pp. 6-12.

The authors address three questions: (1) Is the team always best for the job? (2) What happens when teams fail? and (3) What is management's role in team success or failure? Four factors found to be critical in NPD teams included appropriate team leadership, membership, evolution, and dynamics; appropriate team type; strong team sponsorship; and organizational linkages and support systems (p. 8). The authors conclude that the decision to use teams is just the beginning — management must establish the systems and vision needed to help people work together (p. 12).

X. Michael Song, Sabrina M. Neeley, and Yuzhen, "Managing R&D - Marketing Integration in the New Product Development Process," *Industrial Marketing Management,* Vol. 25, No. 6 (1996), pp. 545-553.

This article reports on an empirical study regarding the coordination of marketing and R&D in new product success. Two factors were found that increase the probability of new product success.

They are (a) a formalized system of procedural interaction, the quality of cross-functional relationship, and a joint-rewards structure contribute to information exchange, (b) the quantity and quality of cross-functional information exchanges are influenced negatively by the lack of credibility, and (c) the quantity and quality of cross-functional information exchanges are influenced positively by rewards for interaction and a high quality of cross-functional relationship.

The roles of purchasing and suppliers are not discussed in this article.

William E. Souder, "Managing Relations Between R&D and Marketing in New Product Development Projects," *The Journal of Product Innovation Management,* Vol. 5, No. 1 (March 1988), pp. 6-19.

This article focuses on disharmony within the R&D/marketing interface in NPD. Characteristics of mild disharmony states were: (1) lack of interaction, (2) lack of communication, and (3) too-good friends. Characteristics of severe disharmony states were: (1) lack of appreciation and (2) distrust. Characteristics of harmony states were (1) equal partner harmony and (2) dominant partner harmony.

The effects of disharmony on NPD success and guidelines for overcoming disharmony are discussed (pp. 12-14): (1) break large projects into smaller ones, (2) take a proactive stance toward interface problems, (3) eliminate mild problems before they grow into severe problems, (4) involve both parties early in the life of the project, (5) promote and maintain dyadic relationships, (6) make open communications an explicit responsibility of everyone, (7) use interlocking task forces, and (8) clarify the decision authorities. An interesting customer-developer conditions (CDC) model is presented (pp. 15-17).

George Stalk, Philip Evans, and Lawrence E. Shulman, "Competing on Capabilities: The New Rules of Corporate Strategy," *Harvard Business Review,* Vol. 70, No. 2 (March-April 1992), pp. 57-69.

"Capabilities-based competition" is an extension of Stalk's previous work on time competitiveness. Four principles of capabilities-based competition are: (1) the building blocks of corporate strategy are business processes, not products and markets; (2) competitive success depends on transforming a company's key processes into strategic capabilities that consistently provide superior value to the customer; (3) companies create these capabilities by making strategic investments in a support infrastructure that links together and transcends traditional SBUs and functions; and (4) because capabilities cross functions, the champion of a capabilities-based strategy is the CEO (p. 62).

The four steps by which a firm becomes a capabilities-based competitor are: (1) shift the strategic framework to achieve aggressive goals, (2) organize around the chosen capability and make sure employees have necessary skills and resources to achieve it, (3) make progress visible and bring measurements and reward into alignment, and (4) do not delegate leadership of the transformation (pp. 64-65).

Capabilities are relatively visible and are broadly based, encompassing the entire value chain. Core competencies emphasize technological and production expertise at specific points along the value chain and are rarely visible. The combination of core competencies and capacities may define the universal model for corporate strategy in the 1990s and beyond (p. 66). This article ties in with the work of Michael Porter and George Day.

Simon J. Towner, "Four Ways to Accelerate New Product Development," *Long-Range Planning,* Vol. 27, No. 2 (1994), pp. 57-65.

The author identifies four strategies for reducing NPD time to market (pp. 60-61): (1) streamline each stage of development, (2) undertake development activities in parallel, (3) launch the product simultaneously in world markets, and (4) release upgrades in product design, service support, and business processes after the launch.

Six key procedures that should be followed to accelerate NPD are: (1) establish an effective governance structure to direct and maintain NPD, (2) appoint a champion to drive the product from R&D to market, (3) establish a program office to integrate development activities, (4) integrate information technology into the process to increase communication and cut time, (5) maintain a focus on business risk to minimize and control company exposure, and (6) test and keep testing to ensure the product and business process work (pp. 62-65).

William J. Walsh, "Get the Whole Organization Behind New Product Development," *Research Technology Management,* Vol. 33, No. 6 (November/December 1990), pp. 32-36.

Organizationally-driven NPD is built around four basic concepts: (1) a holistic approach involving all functional departments, (2) date making and date keeping, (3) individual commitment based on education and training, and (4) program control by means of a New Product Integration Manager. The article contains no mention of supplier involvement.

III. SOURCES IMPORTANT TO PROCESS DEVELOPMENT/IMPROVEMENT

Lance Dixon, "JIT II at Honeywell," *Purchasing,* Vol. 116, No. 2 (February 17, 1994), p. 22.

JIT II relationships build on purchasing techniques of pooling of requirements, establishment of corporate-wide agreements, and strategic supplier relationships at multiple locations. On-site supplier empowerment includes PO authority. Many benefits have resulted from JIT II.

Lance Dixon, "JIT II at KeyCorp," *Purchasing,* Vol. 117, No. 1 (July 14, 1994), p. 37.

This article discusses the process of selecting and working with an on-site supplier of computer equipment, software, maintenance, and training at 800 sites. A buying team comprising personnel from information systems and purchasing was used.

Lance Dixon, "JIT II at Techsonic," *Purchasing,* Vol. 117, No. 5 (October 6, 1994), p. 22.

Techsonic practices a form of JIT II for hardware purchases. Inventory is consigned until used and the supplier serves as an off-site buyer.

Jason R. Lemon, "A Structured Approach to Concurrent Product/Process Development," *Manufacturing Systems,* Vol. 9, No. 6 (June 1991), pp. 32-39.

The author discusses Concurrent Product and Process Development (CP/PD) as an approach to improve quality, reduce overall product costs, shorten time-to-market, reduce product and process development costs, reduce capital investment, and lower overall business risk. Organization and processes of CP/PD are presented.

Gary P. Pisano and Steven C. Wheelwright, "The New Logic of High-Tech R&D," *Harvard Business Review,* Vol. 73, No. 5 (September-October 1995), pp. 93-105.

The authors argue that is necessary to simultaneously develop new products and new processes. Benefits of making process development and process innovation a priority include accelerated time-to-market, rapid ramp-up, and enhanced product functionality and customer acceptance.

Forces driving the strategic value of process-development capabilities include (a) shorter product life cycle, (b) increasingly hard-to-manufacture product designs, (c) fragmented, demanding markets, and (a) growing technological parity. No mention is made of purchasing's role in this article.

Patrick Ponticel, "Integrated Product Process Development," *Automotive Engineering,* Vol. 104, No. 10 (October 1996), pp.103-105.

This article discusses concurrent engineering in which product and process development are integrated. According to the article, early involvement of system suppliers may help define the product for improved manufacturability, recommend flexible processing equipment, and recommend in-process tolerances that may save on equipment costs. No mention is made of purchasing's role in this article.

APPENDIX II: QUESTIONNAIRES AND LETTERS •

The appendix includes:

1. The following items for the "Early Supplier Involvement in New Product Development" study:

   a. "Early Supplier Involvement in New Product Development Questionnaire"

   b. Prenotification letter dated February 3, 1997

   c. Cover letter dated February 10, 1997

   d. Follow-up letter dated February 17, 1997

2. The following items for the "Purchasing Involvement in Production Process Development and Improvement" study:

   a. "Purchasing Involvement in Production Process Development and Improvement Questionnaire"

   b. Prenotification letter dated March 24, 1997

   c. Cover letter dated March 31, 1997

   d. Follow-up letter dated April 7, 1997

EARLY SUPPLIER INVOLVEMENT IN NEW PRODUCT DEVELOPMENT
QUESTIONNAIRE

The purpose of this questionnaire is to study supplier involvement in new product development. This study will increase the understanding of new product development processes and provide useful insights to practitioners and scholars alike.

IF YOU WOULD LIKE A SUMMARY OF THIS STUDY'S RESULTS, PLEASE COMPLETE THE FORM AT THE END OF THE QUESTIONNAIRE ON PAGE 6. IF YOU PREFER ANONYMITY, RETURN THE FORM UNDER SEPARATE COVER.

There are no "right" or "wrong" answers to any of these questions. What is needed is your frank and honest response. You **DO NOT NEED TO LOOK UP ANY INFORMATION IN YOUR COMPANY'S RECORDS.** Answers based on your perceptions and recollections are all that is needed.

YOUR RESPONSES WILL BE STRICTLY CONFIDENTIAL. YOU OR YOUR FIRM WILL NOT BE IDENTIFIED IN ANY WAY. THE RESULTS OF THE DATA ANALYSIS WILL NOT ENABLE THE READER TO DEDUCE THE IDENTITY OF YOU OR YOUR COMPANY.

Your experience and insight are especially important to this study. Because the sample size is small, every response is important.

"New Product Development" as used in this questionnaire refers to new products being marketed by your business unit to consumers, industrial customers, and/or resellers. **"New Product Development Process"** refers to the procedures that guide the conceptualization, design, engineering, production, and sourcing of a new product.

A. **FOCUS OF THE QUESTIONNAIRE**
   The focus of this questionnaire is your "Business Unit." Business Unit refers to the company or division that you identify with in your job.

B. **PURCHASING'S ROLE IN NEW PRODUCT DEVELOPMENT**
   Please circle the response that best describes the role that the Purchasing Department plays in your Business Unit's New Product Development process. Key:

   SD = Strongly Disagree   A = Agree
    D = Disagree   SA = Strongly Agree
    N = Neither Agree nor Disagree

1. Purchasing plays a major role in the New Product Development Process.   SD D N A SA

2. Purchasing becomes involved in the New Product Development Process at the concept stage.   SD D N A SA

3. Purchasing becomes involved in the New Product Development Process after the concept has been finalized.   SD D N A SA

4. Purchasing becomes involved in the New Product Development Process only after the design has been finalized.   SD D N A SA

5. Purchasing plays an important role in New Product Development cross-functional teams.   SD D N A SA

6. Purchasing takes a leadership role in New Product Development cross-functional teams.   SD   D   N   A   SA

7. Purchasing plays an important role in identifying suppliers that offer technologies that give our Business Unit competitive advantages.   SD   D   N   A   SA

8. In our Business Unit, the "typical" new product meets or exceeds its sales objectives.   SD   D   N   A   SA

9. In our Business Unit, the "typical" new product meets or exceeds its profit objectives.   SD   D   N   A   SA

10. In our Business Unit, the "typical" new product meets or beats its time-to-market schedule.   SD   D   N   A   SA

11. Do suppliers participate in the New Product Development Process in your Business Unit? YES_____ NO_____ IF "YES," GO TO PART C. IF "NO," SKIP SECTIONS C AND D, AND GO TO PART E

C.   **THE SUPPLIER'S ROLE IN NEW PRODUCT DEVELOPMENT**
Please circle the response that best reflects your Business Unit's policies/practices regarding supplier participation in its New Product Development Process. Key:

SD = Strongly Disagree   A = Agree
 D = Disagree   SA = Strongly Agree
 N = Neither Agree nor Disagree

12. When used, our suppliers play an important role in the design and development of new products.   SD   D   N   A   SA

13. Suppliers are used frequently for New Product Development.   SD   D   N   A   SA

14. When used, suppliers usually become involved in the New Product Development Process at the concept stage.   SD   D   N   A   SA

15. When used, suppliers usually become involved in the New Product Development Process after the concept has been finalized.   SD   D   N   A   SA

16. When used, suppliers usually become involved in the New Product Development Process after the design has been finalized.   SD   D   N   A   SA

17. Supplier efforts are closely coordinated with our Business Unit's New Product Development Process.   SD   D   N   A   SA

18. Integration of a supplier into the New Product Development Process in our Business Unit happens only if that supplier's top management team is committed to their involvement.   SD   D   N   A   SA

19. Supplier integration into the New Product Development Process is carefully controlled in our Business Unit.   SD   D   N   A   SA

20. Our Business Unit carefully evaluates whether new   SD   D   N   A   SA
    technology is better developed by ourselves or
    with a supplier.

21. Our Business Unit carefully evaluates whether new   SD   D   N   A   SA
    product time-to-market objectives can best be
    achieved by ourselves or with a supplier.

22. Our Business Unit carefully evaluates whether new   SD   D   N   A   SA
    product quality objectives can best be achieved by
    ourselves or with a supplier.

23. There must be a high level of familiarity with a   SD   D   N   A   SA
    supplier's capabilities before it is included in
    our Business Unit's New Product Development Process.

24. The New Product Development process in our   SD   D   N   A   SA
    Business Unit is very receptive to ideas that
    come from our suppliers.

25. The commitment of our Business Unit's top   SD   D   N   A   SA
    management is needed to include a specific
    supplier in our New Product Development Process.

26. There has to be a strong consensus within our   SD   D   N   A   SA
    Business Unit before a specific supplier is
    included in our New Product Development Process.

27. Supplier integration into our New Product   SD   D   N   A   SA
    Development Process results in reduced time-
    to-market of new products.

28. Supplier integration into our New Product   SD   D   N   A   SA
    Development Process results in higher product
    quality.

29. Suppliers are more likely to be integrated into   SD   D   N   A   SA
    New Product Development processes when the
    project is technologically complex.

30. Suppliers share in cost savings they identify   SD   D   N   A   SA
    during the New Product Development Process.

31. Our Business Unit works closely with suppliers to   SD   D   N   A   SA
    achieve target cost objectives during the New
    Product Development Process.

D. **PRACTICES REGARDING SUPPLIER INVOLVEMENT IN NEW PRODUCT DEVELOPMENT**
Please circle the response that best describes the extent to which the following practices are used regarding supplier participation in your Business Unit's New Product Development Process. Key:

1 = Never Used
2 = Almost Never Used
3 = Seldom Used
4 = Occasionally Used

5 = Used More Often Than Not
6 = Used In Most Situation
7 = Very Extensively Used

		Never Used						Very Extensively Used
32.	Supplier membership/participation on your Business Unit's New Product Development project team.	1	2	3	4	5	6	7
33.	Direct cross-functional, inter-company communications between your Business Unit and suppliers.	1	2	3	4	5	6	7
34.	Shared education and training programs between your Business Unit and suppliers.	1	2	3	4	5	6	7
35.	Linked (EDI, CAD/CAM, e-mail) information systems.	1	2	3	4	5	6	7
36.	Co-location of Business Unit and supplier personnel.	1	2	3	4	5	6	7
37.	Frequent technology information sharing between your Business Unit and its suppliers on an "as needed" basis.	1	2	3	4	5	6	7
38.	Training program in mutual trust development.	1	2	3	4	5	6	7
39.	Sharing customer requirements with suppliers.	1	2	3	4	5	6	7
40.	Frequent and detailed sharing of product and process technology information between your Business Unit and its suppliers.	1	2	3	4	5	6	7
41.	Shared physical assets (plant and equipment) between suppliers and your Business Unit.	1	2	3	4	5	6	7
42.	Formalized risk/reward sharing agreements between your Business Unit and suppliers.	1	2	3	4	5	6	7
43.	Joint agreement on performance measurements of the New Product Development Process.	1	2	3	4	5	6	7
44.	Business Unit cross-functional teams for supplier selection and planning.	1	2	3	4	5	6	7
45.	Formal processes for selecting suppliers to be integrated into the New Product Development process.	1	2	3	4	5	6	7

E. COMPETITIVE ENVIRONMENT
Please circle the response that best describes your Business Unit's competitive environment. Key:

SD = Strongly Disagree   A = Agree
 D = Disagree   SA = Strongly Agree
 N = Neither Agree nor Disagree

46. My Business Unit responds quickly and effectively   SD D N A SA
    to changing customer or supplier needs compared to
    our competition.

47. My Business Unit responds quickly and effectively   SD D N A SA
    to changing competitor strategies compared to our
    competitors.

48. My Business Unit develops and markets new products   SD D N A SA
    quickly and effectively compared to our competitors.

49. In most of its markets my Business Unit is a very   SD D N A SA
    strong competitor.

50. In the markets served by my Business Unit, the firm   SD D N A SA
    that eases up usually loses markets/customers to
    its competitors.

51. Competition in the markets served by our Business   SD D N A SA
    Unit is severe.

F. GENERAL INFORMATION
52. Please check the category that best describes the industry that your
    Business Unit is in:

    _____ Food and Kindred Products
    _____ Chemical and Allied Products
    _____ Fabricated Metal Products
    _____ Machinery, Except Electrical
    _____ Electric/Electronic Equipment
    _____ Transportation Equipment
    _____ Miscellaneous Manufacturing Industries
    _____ Gas, Electric, and Sanitary Services
    _____ Other - please specify _____

53. Approximately how many individuals are employed by your Business Unit?
    a. Not including temporary or contract employees. _____
    b. Including temporary or contract employees. _____

54. What was the approximate annual dollar sales last year of your Business
    Unit? _____

55. Ownership of my Business Unit (or parent company) is based in (check the
    appropriate response):
    _____United States
    _____England
    _____Germany
    _____Japan
    _____Canada
    _____Other, please indicate the country_____

56. Approximately how many years' experience do you have in purchasing? Please check the appropriate response.
_____Less than one year; _____1-5 Years; _____6-10 Years
_____11-15 Years; _____16-20 Years; _____Over 20 years

57. Do you have any professional certifications? Please check all that apply.
_____C.P.M.; _____A.P.P.; _____Other, please specify_____

THANK YOU FOR YOUR PARTICIPATION IN THIS RESEARCH!

If you would like a summary of the results of this study, please write your name, address, and telephone number below--or if you prefer--attach your business card. THANK YOU for your cooperation.

Name_____

Address_____

_____

_____

_____

Telephone Number_____

TO RETURN THE QUESTIONNAIRE, please use the enclosed self-addressed business reply envelope, or mail to:

Professor Michael A. McGinnis, C.P.M.
Department of Marketing and Transportation
University of South Alabama
Mobile, Alabama 36688-0002,

or fax to (334) 460-7909

ANY QUESTIONS? PLEASE CALL ME:
(334)460-7907, FAX (334) 460-7909

UNIVERSITY OF SOUTH ALABAMA

DEPARTMENT OF
MARKETING AND TRANSPORTATION
COLLEGE OF
BUSINESS AND MANAGEMENT STUDIES

307 N. UNIVERSITY BLVD.
MOBILE, ALABAMA 36688-0002
TELEPHONE: (334) 460-6412
FAX: (334) 460-7909

February 3, 1997

Dear Purchasing Executive:

I need your help! I am conducting a research project for the Center for Advanced Purchasing Studies (CAPS). CAPS is an affiliation agreement between the National Association of Purchasing Management and Arizona State University. This research addresses the roles of purchasing and suppliers in new product development. You have been selected as part of a random sample of purchasing executives.

In about a week you will receive a questionnaire. Please take a few minutes to complete it. A summary of the results of this study will be available to those who complete the questionnaire.

You will not need to look up any information to complete this questionnaire. Answers based on your perceptions and recollections will be all that is needed. Your participation in this research is confidential, and the results of this study will not reveal information specific to you or your firm in any way.

Since the sample is very small, **your response will be very important**. Thank you in advance for your cooperation.

Sincerely,

Michael A. McGinnis, C.P.M.
Professor of Marketing
 and Logistics

UNIVERSITY OF SOUTH ALABAMA

DEPARTMENT OF
MARKETING AND TRANSPORTATION
COLLEGE OF
BUSINESS AND MANAGEMENT STUDIES

307 N. UNIVERSITY BLVD.
MOBILE, ALABAMA 36688-0002
TELEPHONE: (334) 460-6412
FAX: (334) 460-7909

February 10, 1997

Dear Purchasing Executive:

I need your help! The enclosed questionnaire is part of a research project that I am conducting for the Center for Advanced Purchasing Studies (CAPS). CAPS is an affiliation agreement between the National Association of Purchasing Management and Arizona State University. The research addresses the roles of purchasing and suppliers in new product development. You have been selected as part of a random sample of purchasing executives.

You will not need to look up any information to complete this questionnaire. Answers based on your perceptions and recollections are all that is needed. Your participation in this research is confidential. Your responses will be used for statistical purposes only. In no way will the results of this study reveal information specific to you or your firm.

Because your experience and insights are extremely valuable to the success of this research, please take a few minutes to complete the enclosed questionnaire **by February 17, 1997**. You may return the completed questionnaire in the enclosed postage prepaid envelope.

Since the sample is very small, **your response is important** to the research. To receive a summary of this study, simply complete the form at the end of the questionnaire.

Sincerely,

Michael A. McGinnis, C.P.M.
Professor of Marketing
 and Logistics

Enclosures

UNIVERSITY OF SOUTH ALABAMA

DEPARTMENT OF
MARKETING AND TRANSPORTATION
COLLEGE OF
BUSINESS AND MANAGEMENT STUDIES

307 N. UNIVERSITY BLVD.
MOBILE, ALABAMA 36688-0002
TELEPHONE: (334) 460-6412
FAX: (334) 460-7909

February 17, 1997

Dear Purchasing Executive:

Last week I sent you a questionnaire that addresses the roles of purchasing and suppliers in new product development.

If you have completed the questionnaire, thank you for your cooperation! If not, please take a few minutes of your valuable time to do so now.

If you have misplaced your copy of the questionnaire please call me at (334) 460-7907, or fax your name and address to me at (334) 460-7909.

Because your experience and insights are extremely valuable to this research, please take a few minutes to complete the questionnaire and return it in the postage prepaid envelope.

In appreciation of your participation in this questionnaire I will send you a summary of the results.

Thank you for your valuable time and cooperation.

Sincerely,

Michael A. McGinnis, C.P.M.
Professor of Marketing
 and Logistics.

PURCHASING INVOLVEMENT IN
PRODUCTION PROCESS DEVELOPMENT AND IMPROVEMENT
QUESTIONNAIRE

The purpose of this questionnaire is to study purchasing and supplier involvement in production process development and improvement. This study will increase the understanding of production process development/ improvement and provide useful insights to practitioners and scholars alike.

IF YOU WOULD LIKE A SUMMARY OF THIS STUDY'S RESULTS, PLEASE COMPLETE THE FORM AT THE END OF THE QUESTIONNAIRE ON PAGE 5. IF YOU PREFER ANONYMITY, RETURN THE FORM UNDER SEPARATE COVER.

There are no "right" or "wrong" answers to any of these questions. What is needed is your frank and honest response. You **DO NOT NEED TO LOOK UP ANY INFORMATION IN YOUR COMPANY'S RECORDS.** Answers based on your perceptions and recollections are all that is needed.

YOUR RESPONSES WILL BE STRICTLY CONFIDENTIAL. YOU OR YOUR FIRM WILL NOT BE IDENTIFIED IN ANY WAY. THE RESULTS OF THE DATA ANALYSIS WILL NOT ENABLE THE READER TO DEDUCE THE IDENTITY OF YOU OR YOUR COMPANY.

Your experience and insight are especially important to this study. Because the sample size is small, every response is important.

A. **FOCUS OF THE QUESTIONNAIRE**
    The focus of this questionnaire is your **"Business Unit."** Business Unit refers to the company or division that you identify with in your job.

    "Process" as used in this questionnaire refers to any production/ operations process that uses materials and supplies, capital equipment, labor, and information to convert inputs into products/services.

    "Process Development/Improvement" refers to the procedures that guide the conceptualization, design, engineering, manufacturing, and implementation of changes to production/operations processes.

B. **PROCESSES IN YOUR BUSINESS UNIT**

    Please circle the response that best describes your perceptions regarding processes in your Business Unit. Key:
    SD = Strongly Disagree   A = Agree
    D = Disagree   SA = Strongly Agree
    N = Neither Agree nor Disagree

1. In my Business Unit, processes are a source   SD D N A SA
    of cost advantage.

2. In my Business Unit, processes are a source   SD D N A SA
    of quality advantage.

3. The processes of my Business Unit contribute to   SD D N A SA
    meeting or beating new product time-to-market
    schedules.

4. Process Development/Improvement is a high   SD D N A SA
    priority in my Business Unit.

5. Process Development/Improvement is a high   SD   D   N   A   SA
    priority in my Business Unit for existing products.

6. Those responsible for Process Development/   SD   D   N   A   SA
    Improvement in my Business Unit have a
    "not invented here" mentality.

7. In my Business Unit, Process Development/   SD   D   N   A   SA
    Improvement is more important than New Product
    Development.

8. In my Business Unit, purchasing has the skills   SD   D   N   A   SA
    and knowledge to contribute effectively to
    process development/improvement.

9. **DOES PURCHASING PARTICIPATE IN NEW PROCESS DEVELOPMENT/IMPROVEMENT IN YOUR BUSINESS UNIT? YES_____ NO_____ IF "YES," GO TO PART C. IF "NO," GO TO QUESTION #17**

C. **PURCHASING'S ROLE IN PROCESS DEVELOPMENT/IMPROVEMENT**

    Please circle the response that best describes the role that the Purchasing Department plays in Process Development/Improvement in your Business Unit. Key:

    SD = Strongly Disagree   A = Agree
     D = Disagree   SA = Strongly Agree
     N = Neither Agree nor Disagree

10. Purchasing plays a major role in Process   SD   D   N   A   SA
    Development/Improvement.

11. Purchasing is constantly involved in Process   SD   D   N   A   SA
    Development/Improvement.

12. Purchasing becomes involved in Process   SD   D   N   A   SA
    Development/Improvement only after most of the
    design decisions have been finalized.

13. Purchasing plays an important role in Process   SD   D   N   A   SA
    Development/Improvement cross-functional teams.

14. Purchasing takes a leadership role in Process   SD   D   N   A   SA
    Development/Improvement cross-functional teams.

15. Purchasing plays an important role in identifying   SD   D   N   A   SA
    technologies that are important to Process
    Development/Improvement.

16. Purchasing plays an important role in identifying   SD   D   N   A   SA
    suppliers that are important to Process
    Development/Improvement.

17. **DO SUPPLIERS PARTICIPATE IN THE PROCESS DEVELOPMENT/IMPROVEMENT PROCESS IN YOUR BUSINESS UNIT? YES_____ NO_____ IF "YES," GO TO PART D ON PAGE 3. IF "NO," GO TO PART E ON PAGE 4.**

D. THE SUPPLIER'S ROLE IN PROCESS DEVELOPMENT/IMPROVEMENT

Please circle the response that best reflects your Business Unit's policies/practices regarding supplier participation in Process Development/Improvement. Key:

SD = Strongly Disagree   A = Agree
D = Disagree   SA = Strongly Agree
N = Neither Agree nor Disagree

18. Suppliers are used frequently for Process Development/Improvement.   SD D N A SA

19. When used, suppliers become involved in Process Development/Improvement at the concept stage.   SD D N A SA

20. When used, suppliers become involved in Process Development/Improvement after the concept has been finalized.   SD D N A SA

21. When used, suppliers become involved in Process Development/Improvement after the design has been finalized.   SD D N A SA

22. Supplier efforts are closely coordinated with Process Development/Improvement in my Business Unit.   SD D N A SA

23. Integration of a supplier into Process Development/Improvement happens only if that supplier's top management is committed.   SD D N A SA

24. Supplier integration into Process Development/Improvement is carefully controlled in my Business Unit.   SD D N A SA

25. Our Business Unit carefully evaluates whether new process technology is better developed by ourselves or with a supplier.   SD D N A SA

26. Our Business Unit carefully evaluates whether process quality objectives are better met by ourselves or with a supplier.   SD D N A SA

27. There must be a high level of familiarity with a supplier's capabilities before the supplier is included in Process Development/Improvement.   SD D N A SA

28. Those responsible for Process Development/Improvement in my Business Unit are very receptive to ideas that come from our suppliers.   SD D N A SA

29. The commitment of our Business Unit's top management is needed to include a specific supplier in Process Development/Improvement.   SD D N A SA

30. There has to be a strong consensus within our   SD D N A SA
    Business Unit before a specific supplier is
    included in Process Development/Improvement.

31. Supplier integration into Process Development/   SD D N A SA
    Improvement results in reduced-time-to market of
    new products.

32. Supplier integration into Process Development/   SD D N A SA
    Improvement results in higher product quality in
    my Business Unit.

33. Suppliers are more likely to be integrated into   SD D N A SA
    Process Development/Improvement when the project
    is technologically complex.

34. Suppliers share in cost savings they identify in   SD D N A SA
    Process Development/Improvement projects.

35. My Business Unit works closely with suppliers to   SD D N A SA
    achieve target cost objectives during Process
    Development/Improvement projects.

36. There are on-site supplier personnel in my Business SD D N A SA
    Unit who are assigned full-time to process
    development/improvement.

E.   **COMPETITIVE ENVIRONMENT**

      Please circle the response that best describes your Business Unit's
      competitive environment. Key:

      SD = Strongly Disagree   A = Agree
       D = Disagree   SA = Strongly Agree
       N = Neither Agree nor Disagree

37. My Business Unit responds more quickly and   SD D N A SA
    effectively to customer or supplier changing
    needs than does our competition.

38. My Business Unit responds more quickly and   SD D N A SA
    effectively to changing competitor strategies
    than do   our competitors.

39. My Business Unit develops and markets new products SD D N A SA
    more quickly and effectively than our competitors.

40. In most of its markets, my Business Unit is a very SD D N A SA
    strong competitor.

41. In the markets served by my Business Unit, the firm SD D N A SA
    that eases up usually loses markets/customers to
    its competitors.

42. Competition in the markets served by our Business SD D N A SA
    Unit is severe.

F. GENERAL INFORMATION

43. Please check the one category that best describes the industry that your Business Unit is in:

_____ Food and Kindred Products
_____ Chemical and Allied Products
_____ Fabricated Metal Products
_____ Machinery, Except Electrical
_____ Electric/Electronic Equipment
_____ Transportation Equipment
_____ Miscellaneous Manufacturing Industries
_____ Gas, Electric, and Sanitary Services
_____ Other - please specify _____

44. Approximately how many individuals are employed by your Business Unit?
    a. Not including temporary or contract employees. _____
    b. Including temporary or contract employees. _____

45. What was the approximate annual dollar sales last year of your Business Unit? _____

46. Ownership of my Business Unit (or parent company) is based in (check the appropriate response):
    _____United States
    _____England
    _____Germany
    _____Japan
    _____Canada
    _____Other, please indicate the country_____.

47. Approximately how many years' experience do you have in purchasing? Please check the appropriate response.
    _____Less than one year;   _____1-5 Years;   _____6-10 Years
    _____11-15 Years;   _____16-20 Years;   _____Over 20 years

48. Do you have any professional certifications? Please check all that apply.
    _____C.P.M.; _____A.P.P.; _____Other, please specify_____

THANK YOU FOR YOUR PARTICIPATION IN THIS RESEARCH!

If you would like a summary of the results of this study, please write your name, address, and telephone number below--or if you prefer--attach your business card. **THANK YOU** for your cooperation.

Name_____

Address_____

_____

_____

_____

Telephone Number_____

TO RETURN THE QUESTIONNAIRE, please use the enclosed self-addressed business reply envelope, or mail to:

Dr. Michael A. McGinnis, C.P.M.
Department of Marketing and Transportation
University of South Alabama
Mobile, Alabama 36688-0002,

or fax to (334) 460-7909

ANY QUESTIONS? PLEASE CALL ME:
(334)460-7907, FAX (334) 460-7909

UNIVERSITY OF SOUTH ALABAMA

DEPARTMENT OF
MARKETING AND TRANSPORTATION
COLLEGE OF
BUSINESS AND MANAGEMENT STUDIES

307 N. UNIVERSITY BLVD.
MOBILE, ALABAMA 36688-0002
TELEPHONE: (334) 460-6412
FAX: (334) 460-7909

March 24, 1997

Dear Purchasing Executive:

I need your help! I am conducting a research project for the Center for Advanced Purchasing Studies (CAPS). CAPS is an affiliation agreement between the National Association of Purchasing Management and Arizona State University. This research addresses the roles of purchasing and suppliers in production and process development. You have been selected as part of a random sample of purchasing executives.

In about a week you will receive a questionnaire. Please take a few minutes to complete it. A summary of the results of this study will be available to those who complete the questionnaire.

You will not need to look up any information to complete this questionnaire. Answers based on your perceptions and recollections will be all that is needed. Your participation in this research is confidential, and the results of this study will not reveal information specific to you or your firm in any way.

Since the sample is very small, **your response will be very important.** Thank you in advance for your cooperation.

Sincerely,

Michael A. McGinnis, C.P.M.
Professor of Marketing
 and Logistics

UNIVERSITY OF SOUTH ALABAMA

DEPARTMENT OF
MARKETING AND TRANSPORTATION
COLLEGE OF
BUSINESS AND MANAGEMENT STUDIES

307 N. UNIVERSITY BLVD.
MOBILE, ALABAMA 36688-0002
TELEPHONE: (334) 460-6412
FAX: (334) 460-7909

March 31, 1997

Dear Purchasing Executive:

I need your help! The enclosed questionnaire is part of a research project that I am conducting for the Center for Advanced Purchasing Studies (CAPS). CAPS is an affiliation agreement between the National Association of Purchasing Management and Arizona State University. The research addresses the roles of purchasing and suppliers in production process development. You have been selected as part of a random sample of purchasing executives.

You will not need to look up any information to complete this questionnaire. Answers based on your perceptions and recollections are all that is needed. Your participation in this research is confidential. Your responses will be used for statistical purposes only. In no way will the results of this study reveal information specific to you or your firm.

Because your experience and insights are extremely valuable to the success of this research, please take a few minutes to complete the enclosed questionnaire at your earliest convenience. You may return the completed questionnaire in the enclosed postage prepaid envelope.

Since the sample is very small, **your response is important** to the research. To receive a summary of this study, simply complete the form at the end of the questionnaire.

If you have any questions please contact met at (334) 460-7907 or fax (334) 460-7909.

Sincerely,

Michael A. McGinnis, C.P.M.
Professor of Marketing
 and Logistics

Enclosures

UNIVERSITY OF SOUTH ALABAMA

DEPARTMENT OF
MARKETING AND TRANSPORTATION
COLLEGE OF
BUSINESS AND MANAGEMENT STUDIES

307 N. UNIVERSITY BLVD.
MOBILE, ALABAMA 36688-0002
TELEPHONE: (334) 460-6412
FAX: (334) 460-7909

April 7, 1997

Dear Purchasing Executive:

Last week I sent you a questionnaire that addresses the roles of purchasing and suppliers in production process development.

If you have completed the questionnaire, thank you for your cooperation! If not, please take a few minutes of your valuable time to do so now.

If you have misplaced your copy of the questionnaire, please call me at (334) 460-7907, or fax your name and address to me at (334) 460-7909. I will be happy to send you another questionnaire.

Because your experience and insights are extremely valuable to this research, please take a few minutes to complete the questionnaire and return it in the postage prepaid envelope.

In appreciation of your participation in this questionnaire I will send you a summary of the results.

Thank you for your valuable time and cooperation.

Sincerely,

Michael A. McGinnis, C.P.M.
Professor of Marketing
 and Logistics.

APPENDIX III: STUDY A: EARLY SUPPLIER INVOLVEMENT IN NEW PRODUCT DEVELOPMENT •

METHODOLOGY AND RESULTS

Methodology

The methodology section describes the techniques used to gather the data used in the study. It provides a means for the technically inclined reader to develop an in-depth understanding of the research techniques used to develop results and recommendations contained in this study.

Questionnaire Development

A six page, 57-item questionnaire was developed to gather data regarding purchasing's role in new product development, the supplier's role in new product development, practices regarding supplier involvement in new product development, the competitive environment, and general information.

Please see annotated bibliography for references. The questionnaire, pre-notification letter, cover letter, and follow-up letter are shown in Appendix II.

The questionnaire focused on ten research issues. The classification of questionnaire items relevant to the research issues were as follows:

RESEARCH ISSUE	NUMBER OF QUESTIONNAIRE ITEMS
1. Early Supplier Involvement	6
2. Role of Purchasing	7
3. Supplier Identification/Certification	8
4. Timing of Involvement	4
5. Technology/Information Sharing	3
6. Monitoring and Control	8
7. Risk/Reward Sharing	3
8. Time/Quality Savings	3
9. The Business Unit and Its Market	13
10. Respondent Information	2

The questionnaire was organized into six sections: Focus of the questionnaire (Section A), Purchasing's Role in New Product Development (Section B), The Supplier's Role in New Product Development (Section C), Practices Regarding Supplier Development in New Product Development (Section D), Competitive Environment (Section E), and General Information (Section F).

Items 18, 23, 25, and 26 in Section C represented "project environmental factors," taken from a Michigan State University study, that distinguish between "most successful" and "least successful" new product development projects. Section D (items 32 - 45) represented "management practices," taken from a Michigan State University study, that distinguish between "most successful" and "least successful" new product development projects. The purpose of using these items was to replicate the findings of that research.

Sampling and Response Analysis

A random sample of 1,051 National Association of Purchasing Management (NAPM) members in NAPM's "Title 1" (purchasing senior management) membership list was selected from the 50 United States. A prenotification letter was mailed to each individual one week prior to mailing the questionnaire and cover letter. A follow-up letter was sent to each individual one week later. A copy of the questionnaire, prenotification letter, cover letter, and follow-up letter are included in Appendix II.

By the cut-off date for responses, 252 usable responses had been received. The usable response rate of 24.0 percent was deemed adequate for analysis. Analysis of the respondents by industry category indicated that the estimated response rate for manufacturing firms was 43.9 percent, service firms 18.6 percent, and other 8.2 percent. The composition of all respondents was 66.7 percent from manufacturing, 17.9 percent from services, and 13.9 percent from other industry categories. Exhibit A-1 summarizes the questionnaire response rate.

Analysis of the usable responses by ZIP Code, as determined by the postmark on the business reply envelope or the respondents' request for a summary of the results, indicated that the response rate by geographical region did not differ by an amount greater than that due to chance.

Exhibit A-1
EARLY SUPPLIER INVOLVEMENT IN NEW PRODUCT DEVELOPMENT QUESTIONNAIRE
RESPONSE RATES

Industry Category	Population Number/ Percentage	Estimated Number in Sample[1]	Usable Responses/ Usable Response Percent of Estimated Sample	Percentage of Total Respondents
Manufacturing	1274/36.5%	383	168/43.9%	66.7%
Service	804/23.0%	242	45/18.6%	17.9%
Other	1417/40.5%	426	35/8.2%	13.9%
Missing Values	0	0	4/NA	1.6%
Totals	3,495/100%	1,051/100%	252/24.0%	100%

[1]Estimated Number in the Sample = [(Number in the Population)/3,495] x [1,051]

Overall, the respondents reflected the geographical distribution of the sample, were more representative of manufacturing and somewhat less representative of service, and reflected limited representation from other industry categories.

DATA ANALYSIS

Factor Analysis

Factor Analysis is a data reduction technique that enables the researcher to identify underlying ideas, or constructs, contained in a series of questionnaire items. This enables the researcher to (a) simplify a large number of questionnaire items into a smaller number of constructs and (b) identify specific questionnaire items that explicitly describe complex constructs.

The authors felt this technique would be useful because of the limitations of describing data that includes a large number of variables.

Two issues are relevant in this type of analysis. First, do the factors identified make sense? The questions associated with a factor have to make sense if they are to be useful for further analysis. For example, a factor that included apples, oranges, and grapes might be considered "fruit." However, a factor that included apples, fish, and limestone might not make sense for purposes of further analysis. The issue that addresses "Does the factor make sense?" is *validity*. Validity is concerned with how well the factor (or any social science measuring instru-

ment) measures the concept identified in the factor analysis. The issue of validity will be addressed as each factor is discussed.

Second, is the statistical reliability of the factors adequate for further analysis? *Reliability* refers to the internal consistency among (or between) the variables in a factor. Factors with high reliability are more likely to be reproducible in subsequent studies. The measure of reliability used in this research is the reliability coefficient, commonly referred to as the Cronbach's coefficient alpha.

Generally, a factor must make sense (be valid) and have adequate reliability to be useful for purposes of analysis. One factor in the absence of the other does not result in a useful factor.

The statistical package used in this study was **SPSS for Microsoft Windows 6.2.** Principal Components was used with a limiting Eigenvalue of 1.0 or greater for Varimax Rotation. These options maximize internal similarity of factors and minimize the similarity among or between factors.

Factor Analysis of the New Product Development Questionnaire, Section B.

As shown in Exhibit A-2, two factors were identified in Section B. The first factor comprised five questionnaire items. These five items address purchasing's role in the new product development process including stage of involvement, roles in new product development cross-functional teams, and in the identification of suppliers. Examination of the five questions resulted in the name, *Purchasing in a Major New Product Development Role*. The reliability coefficient of 0.8735 was well above the value of 0.70 thought to be adequate for basic research. It was concluded that face validity and reliability of this factor was adequate for use in subsequent analysis.

Three questionnaire items loaded on a second factor. These three items focused on issues of product success: sales success, profitability, and time-to-market. The name for this factor, *New Product Success* reflected the nature of the questionnaire items. The reliability, coefficient of 0.7610 was satisfactory. It was concluded that the face validity and reliability of this factor was adequate for use in subsequent analysis.

The third factor comprised two questionnaire items that related to purchasing's participation in the later stages of the new product development process. *Purchasing in a Minor New Product Development Role* reflected the nature of the two questionnaire items. Because the reliability coefficient for this factor was 0.5922, it was decided not to use this factor in subsequent analysis.

Factor Analysis of the New Product Development Questionnaire, Section C.

As shown in Exhibit A-3, four interpretable factors were identified in Section C. The first factor, *New Product Development Strategic Evaluation and Control,* comprised six questionnaire items and had a reliability coefficient of 0.8680. The six items addressed coordination and control, whether new technology is better developed by a supplier, whether time-to-market objectives can be best achieved with suppliers, whether quality objectives can be achieved with a supplier, and the achievement of target cost objectives.

The second factor was *Supplier's Role in New Product Development*. The reliability coefficient was 0.6922. The three items loading on this factor focused on the importance of the role played by suppliers, frequency of supplier use, and at what point suppliers become involved in the new product development process.

The third factor, *Supplier Integration New Product Development Outcomes,* focused on the results of supplier involvement in the areas of time-to-market and product quality. The coefficient of reliability for this factor was 0.7503. The final usable factor was *Timing of Supplier New Product Development Involvement.* The two items loading on this factor addressed when suppliers become involved in the new product development process. The reliability coefficient was 0.7987.

Two factors from Section C were not used in subsequent analysis. *Early Commitment* had a reliability coefficient of 0.6287. A sixth factor had a low coefficient of reliability and was difficult to interpret.

Factor Analysis of the New Product Development Questionnaire, Section D.

The questionnaire items used in Section D were based on previously used questions associated with successful supplier involvement in new product development. As shown in Exhibit A-4, three interpretable factors were identified. The first factor, *Continuing Commitment,* comprised five items that addressed shared training, location, plant and equipment, and risk/reward between users and suppliers. The coefficient of reliability was 0.8038. The second factor was *Explicit New Product Development Processes.* The coefficient of reliability was 0.8408. The five questions loading on this factor focused on explicit processes between buying and selling organizations in the areas of participation, communications, performance measures, supplier selection, and supplier integration into the new product development process.

The third factor, *Sharing Confidential Information,* comprised three items that focused on sharing of technical and customer information by buyers with suppliers. The reliability coefficient was 0.7598.

Factor Analysis of the New Product Development Questionnaire, Section E.

This factor analysis was conducted to confirm two scales that have been widely used in logistics strategy research. The two factors, *Business Unit Competitive Responsiveness* and *Competitive Hostility,* were identical to the previously used scales. These scales are shown in Exhibit A-5.

Factor Analysis, Development of Factor Scores

Factor scores were calculated for each individual respondent on each of the 11 factors that met the authors' validity and reliability objectives. The factor score is the arithmetic average of all questionnaire items loading on the factor. For example, the factor score for each individual on Factor B-1 would be the sum of that respondent's responses to questionnaire items 1, 2, 5, 6, and 7 divided by five.

Respondent factor scores can be used to divide respondents into "High" and "Low" categories based on their score means, to compare respondent mean scores between two or more categories, or statistically compare relationships among two or more factors.

In the next section, the t-test is used to compare individual factor scores between levels of product success, between respondents who include suppliers in new product development, and between respondents who consider their business units to be *high* on competitive responsiveness and those who are *low* on competitive responsiveness.

T-Tests of Selected Variables

The t-test is a statistical test between the means of two samples. The purpose of this test is to determine if the two means differ by an amount greater than due to chance. For example, if the means of A and B are significantly different at the 0.05 level, it can be concluded that the difference is not merely due to chance variation in the data. Conversely, if the pair is not significantly different at the 0.05 level, it would be concluded that the differences in means are due to chance variations in the data.

In the second stage of the analysis, respondent factor scores on selected factors were divided into "High" and "Low" categories. The statistical t-test was then conducted between high and low categories to ascertain statistical differences between categories and respondent factor scores. The purpose of this analysis was to provide the researchers with insights into factors that might be managerially useful in managing early supplier involvement in new product development. The following sections present these results.

T-test of New Product Success with Selected Factors

Respondents were divided into "High" and "Low" categories based on their New Product Success factor score means. Eight of ten factors were significant at the 0.05 level of significance. These results provide insights into which factors are likely to contribute to new product success.

As shown in Exhibit A-6, the significant factors were:

B-1: Purchasing in a Major New Product Development Role
C-1: Strategic Evaluation and Control
C-3: Supplier Integration Outcomes
D-1: Continuing Commitment
D-2: Explicit Processes
D-3: Sharing Confidential Information
E-1: Business Unit Competitive Responsiveness
E-2: Competitive Hostility

Respondent factor scores of the following two factors did not differ significantly at the 0.05 level:

C-2: Supplier's Role in New Product Development
C-5: Timing of Supplier Involvement

Respondents who consider their business units to be above average on product success are more likely to perceive that:

1. Purchasing plays a greater than average role in new product development. This includes becoming involved in new product development at the concept stage, playing an important role in cross-functional new product development teams, and playing an important role in identifying suppliers that offer competitive technology.

2. Supplier involvement in new product development is closely coordinated and controlled by the business unit. This includes evaluating whether new technology, new product time-to-market objectives, and quality objectives can best be achieved solely by the business unit or with a supplier. Finally, these business units work closely with suppliers to achieve target cost objectives.

3. Supplier integration into new product development processes results in reduced time-to-market and higher product quality.

4. There is a greater commitment to the buyer-supplier new product development relationship. This greater commitment incudes shared education and training programs, co-location of supplier and business unit personnel, mutual trust training, shared physical assets, and formalized risk/reward sharing agreements.

5. There is greater level of explicit agreement between the buyer and seller regarding shared membership on new product development project teams; cross-functional, intercompany communications; and joint agreement on performance measures. In addition, the business unit is perceived as being more likely to use cross-functional teams for supplier selection and planning and more likely to have a formal process for selecting suppliers that will be integrated into the new product planning process.

6. They are more likely to share confidential business unit technical and customer information with suppliers.

7. Their business unit is a very strong competitor; is more responsive to changing customer and supplier needs, and competitor strategies; and more likely to develop and market new products better than competitors.

8. Their business unit is in a hostile market.

Respondents who consider their business units to be above average on new product success were not different at the 0.05 level from the respondents who consider themselves below average, in the following areas:

1. The supplier's role in terms of importance, frequency of supplier use, or when the supplier becomes involved in the new product development process.

2. The timing of supplier involvement in the new product development process.

T-test of Supplier Involvement in New Product Development with Selected Factors

These t-tests compare respondents whose suppliers participate in the new product development process (168 respondents) with those who do not (84 respondents). Those respondents whose suppliers participate in the new product development process perceive that purchasing has a larger role in new product development, products are more successful, and the competitive environment is more hostile.

As shown in Exhibit A-7, the following three of four factors were significant at the 0.05 level, according to the t-test:

B-1: Purchasing in a Major New Product Development Role
B-2: New Product Success
E-2: Competitive Hostility

Respondent factor score means did not differ significantly at the 0.05 level on one factor:

E-1: Competitive Responsiveness

Respondents who include suppliers in the new product development process are more likely to perceive that:

1. Purchasing plays a greater than average role in new product development. This includes becoming involved in new product development at the concept stage, playing an important role in cross-functional new product development teams, and playing an important role in identifying suppliers that offer competitive technology.

2. Business unit products are more successful in terms of meeting or exceeding sales objective, profit objectives, and time-to-market schedule.

3. Their business unit is in a hostile market.

Respondents who include suppliers in the new product development process did not differ from those who do not use suppliers in the new product development process in the following area:

1. More likely to perceive their business unit as a very strong competitor by being more responsive to changing customer needs, supplier needs, and competitor strategies; more likely to develop and market new products better than competitors.

T-test of Factor Scores with Business Unit Employment and Sales

This test was performed to ascertain whether or not organizational size affected respondent perceptions regarding the subject of this research.

Based on individual factor scores, the respondents were divided into "High" and "Low" categories on each of the 11 factors. The questionnaire means of items 44a (Number of employees employed by your business unit) and 45 (Approximate annual sales of your business unit last year) for the "High" and "Low" categories of each factor were compared using the t-test.

Of the 22 comparisons, one was significant at the 0.05 level. Number of Employees averaged 1,486 in respondent business units of respondents in the high category of factor C-2: Supplier's Role in New Product Development. The average number of employees in the low category was 7,641. None of the other 21 comparisons were significant at the 0.05 level. It was concluded that business unit size, in terms of employment or revenue, does not substantially affect overall purchasing and supplier involvement in new product development.

Issues That Affect New Product Success: Regression Analysis

A second analysis was conducted to further evaluate the effects of the above variables on new product success. This analysis consisted of a regression analysis using Factor B-2: New Product Success as the dependent variable. One regression analysis was conducted with 156 of 168 respondents who responded that suppliers are involved in new product development in their business unit. A second regression analysis was conducted with 80 of 84 respondents who responded that suppliers are not involved in new product development in their business unit.

The subjects of the first regression analysis were respondents who indicated that suppliers are involved in new product development in their business unit. The following eight independent variables used in this analysis were identified in the previous section as affecting new product success and were relevant to situations in which suppliers are involved in new product development:

B-1: Purchasing in a Major New Product Development Role
C-1: Strategic Evaluation and Control

C-3: Supplier Integration Outcomes
D-1: Continuing Commitment
D-2: Explicit Processes
D-3: Sharing Confidential Information
E-1: Business Unit Competitive Responsiveness
E-2: Competitive Hostility

As shown in Exhibit A-8, the following three independent variables entered the equation for respondents who involve suppliers in new product development:

B-1: Purchasing in a Major New Product Development Role
C-1: New Product Development Strategic Evaluation and Control
E-1: Business Unit Competitive Responsiveness

Factor C-1: Strategic Evaluation and Control explained 18.0 percent of the variance in New Product Success. The contributions of E-1: Business Unit Competitive Responsiveness, and B-1: Purchasing in a Major New Product Development Role to New Product Success variance were 6.5 percent and 3.0 percent respectively. The final equation was (B-2) = 1.208 + 0.219(C-1) + 0.208(E-1) + 0.157(B-1) where scales for B-2, B-1, C-1, and E-1 are: 1 = Strongly Disagree to 5 = Strongly Agree. This equation explained 27.6 percent of the variance in New Product Success. The other 72.4 percent of the variance in New Product Success is explained by other variables such as product features, pricing decisions, promotional efforts, and distribution activities.

When suppliers are involved, three factors are likely to have an essential positive affect on new product success:
1. New Product Development Strategic Evaluation and Control (the careful evaluation of whether suppliers can contribute to technology/time-to-market/quality objectives, careful control of supplier integration into the new product development process, and close coordination of goals and efforts)
2. Business Unit Competitive Responsiveness (organizational commitment to time competitiveness)
3. Purchasing in a Major New Product Development Role (early purchasing participation, contributions to cross-functional teams, and proactive identification of suppliers that can provide technological competitive advantages)

The subjects of the second regression analysis were respondents who indicated that suppliers are not involved in new product development in their business unit. The following three independent variables used in this analysis were previously identified as affecting new product success and were relevant to situations in which suppliers are not involved in new product development:

B-1: Purchasing in a Major New Product Development Role
E-1: Business Unit Competitive Responsiveness
E-2: Competitive Hostility

As shown in Exhibit A-8, one variable entered the equation for respondents who do not involve suppliers in new product development. The variable, E-1: Business Unit Competitive Responsiveness, explained 35.8 percent of the variance in New Product Success. The final equation was (B-2) = 1.355 + 0.487(E-1) where scales for B-2 and E-1 are: 1 = Strongly Disagree to 5 = Strongly Agree. This equation explained 35.8 percent of the variance in New Product Success. The other 64.2 percent of the variance in New Product Success is explained by other variables such as product features, pricing decisions, promotional efforts, and distribution activities.

When suppliers are not involved, one factor is likely to have an essential positive affect on new product success: Business Unit Competitive Responsiveness (organizational commitment to time competitiveness).

Contingency Table Analysis with the Chi-square Statistic of Selected Variables

Contingency table analysis with the chi-square test is used when the variables being analyzed are nominal. For example, comparing respondents classified as *high* and *low* on dimension A and *high* and *low* on dimension B would be an appropriate use of the contingency table analysis. The t-test would not be appropriate in this example because neither of the variables are interval.

In this step of the analysis, the statistical relationships among six nominally scaled variables were evaluated using contingency table analysis with the chi-square statistic. This technique is the nonparametric test for use with nominally scaled data. Interpretation of the results is similar to the t-test. If the observed results differ from the expected results at the 0.05 level, it can be concluded that the differences are greater than what would be expected due to chance. If the results are not significant at the 0.05 level, it would be concluded that differences between observed and expected results do not differ by an amount greater than that due to chance. The six variables analyzed in this step of the analysis were:

1. New Product Success (High, Low)
2. Supplier Participation in New Product Development (Yes, No)
3. Industry Category (Manufacturing, Services, Other)
4. Ownership of Business Unit (United States, Other)
5. Respondent Years of Experience in Purchasing (0-10 Years, 11 Years of More)
6. Professional Certification (One or more professional certifications, No Certification)

Contingency Table Analysis of New Product Success with Selected Variables

Respondents were divided into *high* and *low* categories based on their New Product Success factor scores. Two of the five variables (Supplier Participation in New Product Development, Ownership of the Business Unit) were not independent of Product Success (significant at the 0.05 level). Three variables (Industry Category, Years of Experience in Purchasing, Professional Certification) were independent of Product Success.

As shown in Exhibit A-9, two variables were not independent of New Product Success. Respondents whose business unit includes suppliers in new product development were more likely to perceive product success as being high. Perceived new product success is more likely to be considered as low by respondents whose business unit does not include suppliers in new product development.

Respondents whose business unit was owned by U.S.-based interests were more likely to perceive product success as high.

Three variables were independent of perceived product success. They were industry category, years experience in purchasing, and professional certification. Perceived product success did not differ among manufacturing, service, and other industry categories. Finally, years experience in purchasing or professional certifications did not vary with perceived product success.

Contingency Table Analysis of Supplier Participation in New Product Development

Respondents were divided into Yes and No categories based on their response to questionnaire item 11, "Do suppliers participate in the New Product Development Process in your Business Unit?" Two of four variables (Industry Category, Years Experience in Purchasing) were not independent of Supplier Participation in New Product Development (significant at the 0.05 level). Two variables (Ownership of Business Unit, Professional Certification) were independent of supplier participation in new product development.

As shown in Exhibit A-9, two variables were not independent of supplier participation in new product development. They were industry category and years experience in purchasing. Respondents in manufacturing are more likely to include suppliers in new product development. Respondents in services and other industries are less likely to include suppliers in new product development. Respondents who have 11 or more years experience in purchasing are more likely to include suppliers in new product development than are respondents with 10 or fewer years experience in purchasing.

Two variables were independent of supplier participation in new product development: ownership of the business unit and professional certification. Respondents whose business unit was owned by U.S. interests did not differ in supplier participation in new product development from business units whose ownership was other than the United States. Supplier participation in new product development did not vary with respondent professional certification.

DISCUSSION OF RESULTS

This portion of the report interprets the research results and discusses the implications for purchasing management.

Insights from the Factor Analysis

Factor B-1: Purchasing Plays a Major Role in The New Product Development Process

Five questionnaire items comprise this factor. They address the role played by purchasing in new product development in terms of its importance, timing of involvement, participation in cross-functional teams, and identification of suppliers. These items also provide a reference for what constitutes a major purchasing role in new product development.

This factor is consistent with purchasing's role as seen in the literature. While the activities of purchasing in a major new product development role are consistent with purchasing's normal activities, it may be necessary for some purchasing managers to develop the interpersonal and team skills of the purchasing staff if the department is to maximize its contribution to the new product development process.

Factor B-2: New Product Success

This factor provides a method of quantifying what is meant by "new product success." The three items loading on the factor represent three dimensions of product success discussed in the literature: sales, profitability, and time-to-market. As a result, this factor, if replicated in future research, may provide an efficient means for researchers to quantify product success.

Factor C-1: New Product Development Strategic Evaluation and Control

Six items comprise this factor. The three dimensions — close coordination and control of supplier integration, careful evaluation of objectives, and a focus on cost objectives — described by these items indicate that new product development strategic evaluation and control comprises six interdependent activities. For example, close coordination and controlled integration of suppliers into the new product development process without careful evaluation of whether supplier participation can contribute to business unit goals would be inadequate strategic evaluation and control. Similarly, careful analysis of whether to use suppliers in the new product development process without effective coordination and control is inadequate. The insights developed by this factor are consistent with the new product development literature.

The inclusion of items 20, 21, 22, and 31 in this factor provides insights into the role competitive advantage plays in the new product development process. According to the results of Factor C-1, three items (20, 21, and 22) focus on sources of meaningful differentiation. Focus on cost objective (item 31) is consistent with the other dimension of competitive advantage, low cost producer. Apparently, the components of competitive advantage (low cost producer, meaningful differentiation, or a combination of both) are considered as part of an overall perspective, rather than as separate issues by the respondents.

Overall, this factor provides a perspective in which close coordination, careful control, and careful evaluation are used to achieve business unit competitive advantage.

Factor C-2: Supplier's Role in New Product Development

This factor provides a means of quantifying the supplier's role in the new product development process. The components of this factor address the importance level of the supplier's role, whether suppliers are used frequently, and at what stage of the new product development process they become involved. The reliability of this factor, 0.6922, is acceptable for further analysis.

Factor C-3: Supplier Integration New Product Development Outcomes

This factor is composed of two outcomes of supplier integration into the new product development process. These two issues, time-to-market and product quality, focus on two sources of meaningful differentiation.

Factor C-5: Timing of Supplier New Product Development Involvement

This factor provides a means of evaluating the importance of timing of supplier participation in new product development. The two items loading on this factor focus on supplier involvement at a later stage in the new product development process. As a result a *high* factor score means later involvement and a *low* factor score indicates early involvement.

Factor D-1: Continuing New Product Development Commitment

This factor addresses five issues that relate to ethical issues in long-term buyer-seller relationships. Shared training, personnel location, and physical assets create the potential for misunderstandings and deceptive behavior. Training in mutual trust and formalized risk/reward agreements help to address those problems. This factor also emphasizes the breadth of commitment when the relationship is continuing.

Factor D-2: Explicit New Product Development Processes

This factor focuses on the extent of explicit processes involved in creating and maintaining supplier involvement in new product development. Five items comprise this factor. They address supplier participation in buyer new product development teams, cross-functional/intercompany communications, and joint agreement on performance measures. The fifth item recognizes formal process for supplier selection as part of the overall process. Item 43, joint agreement on performance measurements, addresses an ethical concern in complex buyer-seller relationships (the necessity of preparing explicit agreements to avoid potential misunderstandings).

Factor D-3: Sharing Confidential Information

The three items loading on this factor represent the range of confidential information that is likely to be shared between buyers and sellers who are cooperating on buyer new product development projects. The sharing of confidential information, according to this factor, includes frequent sharing, sharing of customer requirement, and the sharing of product and process technology.

Factor E-1: Business Unit Competitive Responsiveness

This scale provides a means of evaluating the respondent's perception of his/her business unit's time responsiveness. This scale has been used as an independent variable to evaluate logistics strategy. The results of the factor analysis confirmed the stability of this scale.

Factor E-2: Competitive Hostility

This scale is a measure of the external environment faced by the business unit. This scale has been previously used as an independent variable to evaluate logistics strategy. The factor analysis confirmed the stability of this scale.

T-Tests of Selected Variables

The following section interprets the results of the t-tests and discusses their implications for purchasing professionals.

T-test of New Product Success With Selected Factors

Eight of 10 factors were not independent of Factor B-1: New Product Success. These results indicate that an array of new product development strategies were associated with high perceived product success. These strategies included purchasing in a major new product development role; close coordination and control of supplier integration with emphasis on technology, time-to-market, quality, and costs; and substantial amounts of sharing of resources and information accompanied by explicit goals, agreements, and training. The business unit with high perceived product success was substantially more time competitive and faced a competitive environment that was hostile.

T-test of Supplier Involvement in New Product Development With Selected Factors

Business units that are more likely to include suppliers in the new product development process are also more likely to include purchasing in a major role, have products that are more successful, and face hostile competition.

T-test of Factor Scores With Business Unit Employment and Sales

Subject responses to the study did not vary substantially with business unit size in terms of employment or annual sales.

Contingency Table Analysis With the Chi-square Statistic of Selected Variables

This section provides additional insights regarding relationships among product success, supplier participation in new product development, industry category, business unit ownership, respondent years experience in purchasing, and respondent professional certification.

Contingency Table Analysis of New Product Success With Selected Variables

According to Table 1A of Exhibit A-9, 97 of 167 respondents (58.1%) whose business unit includes suppliers in the new product development process perceived new product success as *high*. Only 37 of 83 respondents (44.6%) whose business unit does not include suppliers in the new product development process perceived new product success as *high*. New product success was perceived as higher in U.S.-owned business units, 122 of 215 (56.7%), than in business units owned by interests in other countries, 10 of 29 (34.5%).

Industry category (manufacturing, service, other), respondent years experience in purchasing, and respon-

dent professional certification were all independent of new product success.

These results confirm the earlier t-tests regarding supplier participation and new product success. The results regarding business unit ownership refute any generalization that United States organizations are automatically less successful than foreign-based firms. The independence of new product success with industry category, years experience in purchasing, and professional certification suggests that future studies can discount those variables.

Contingency Table Analysis of Supplier Participation in New Product Development With Selected Variables

Industry category and respondent years experience in purchasing are associated with supplier participation in new product development.

Examination of Table 2A of Exhibit A-9 indicates that manufacturing firms are more likely, 130 of 168 (77.4%), to include suppliers in new product development than service firms, 18 of 46 (40.0%), or firms in "other" industry categories, 17 of 35 (48.6%). While business units in manufacturing firms are more likely to include suppliers in new product development, a substantial minority of nonmanufacturing business units include suppliers in new product development. This finding suggests that there may be unrealized potential for supplier participation in new product development in nonmanufacturing firms.

Examination of Table 2C of Exhibit A-9 reveals that respondents with 11 or more years experience in purchasing, 135 of 188 (71.8%), are more likely to include suppliers in new product development than are respondents with 10 or fewer years experience, 32 of 62 (51.6%). Apparently, purchasing executives with more experience in purchasing (a) have a better understanding of suppliers' potential for contributing to new product development, (b) have better developed supplier management skills, and/or (c) have had more opportunities to work with suppliers on new product development.

Business unit ownership and respondent professional certification were independent of supplier participation in new product development.

Contingency Table Analysis of Industry Category With Selected Variables

Nearly all foreign-owned business units were in manufacturing. Respondent years experience in purchasing and professional certification were independent of industry category.

As shown in Table 3A of Exhibit A-9, only two foreign-owned firms were not in manufacturing — 27 of 166 (16.3%) manufacturing firms were foreign owned. Individual respondent years experience in purchasing and professional certification were independent of industry category.

Overall Insights for the Contingency Table Analysis

The contingency table analysis highlights the interdependency of supplier participation in new product development with perceived new product success, industry category, and years experience in purchasing. Perceived new product success was higher in U.S.-owned business units than in foreign-owned business units. Finally, nearly all foreign-owned business units were in manufacturing.

Respondent years of experience in purchasing and professional certification were not substantial variables in terms of interdependencies with other variables. Industry category and business ownership appeared to be of limited importance in these results.

Regardless of the interdependencies, it should be noted that new product success and supplier participation do occur in all situations studied. This means that the absence of supplier participation in new product development does not necessarily preclude new product success. Further, it should be recognized that the specific variables affecting new product success vary among firms.

While the contingency table analysis identifies interdependance among the variables analayzed, five of 15 interdependancies at the 0.05 level suggests that the practical effects of these variables to practitioners is nil.

FACTOR ANALYSIS OF EARLY SUPPLIER INVOLVEMENT IN NEW PRODUCT
DEVELOPMENT QUESTIONNAIRE: SECTION B

Questionnaire Items	Reliability Coefficients (Alphas)[1]/ % of Variance	Factor Loadings[2]
Factor B-1: PURCHASING IN A MAJOR NEW PRODUCT DEVELOPMENT ROLE	0.8735/ 40.1%	
1. Purchasing plays a major role in the New Product Development Process.		0.8502
2. Purchasing becomes involved in the New Product Development Process at the concept stage.		0.7353
5. Purchasing plays an important role in New Product Development cross-functional teams.		0.8306
6. Purchasing takes a leadership role in New Product Development cross-functional teams.		0.7454
7. Purchasing plays an important role in identifying suppliers that offer technology that gives our Business Unit competitive advantages.		0.7490
Factor B-2: NEW PRODUCT SUCCESS	0.7610/ 16.2%	
8. In our Business Unit, the "typical" new product meets or exceeds its sales objectives.		0.8249
9. In our Business Unit, the "typical" new product meets or exceeds its profit objectives.		0.8803
10. In our Business Unit, the "typical" new product meets or beats its time-to-market schedule.		0.7225
Factor B-3: PURCHASING IN A MINOR NEW PRODUCT DEVELOPMENT ROLE	0.5922/ 11.4%	
3. Purchasing becomes involved in the New Product Development Process after the concept has been finalized.		0.8984
4. Purchasing becomes involved in the New Product Development Process only after the design has been finalized.		0.7026

Total Variance Explained: 69.5%

---

[1]Jum C. Nunnally and Ira H. Bernstein, *Psychometric Theory,* 3rd edition (New York: McGraw-Hill, Inc., 1994), pp. 232-233.
[2]Factor Loadings are the correlations between each variable and each factor.

FACTOR ANALYSIS OF EARLY SUPPLIER INVOLVEMENT IN NEW PRODUCT
DEVELOPMENT QUESTIONNAIRE: SECTION C

Questionnaire Items	Reliability Coefficients (Alphas)[1]/ % of Variance	Factor Loadings[2]
Factor C-1: NEW PRODUCT DEVELOPMENT STRATEGIC EVALUATION AND CONTROL	0.8680/ 29.5%	
17. Supplier efforts are closely coordinated with our Business Unit's New Product Development Process.		0.6248
19. Supplier integration into the New Product Development Process is carefully controlled in our Business Unit.		0.6832
20. Our Business Unit carefully evaluates whether new technology is better developed by ourselves or with a supplier.		0.8644
21. Our Business Unit carefully evaluates whether new product time-to-market objectives can best be achieved by ourselves or with a supplier.		0.8338
22. Our Business Unit carefully evaluates whether new product quality objectives can best be achieved by ourselves or with a supplier.		0.8185
31. Our Business Unit works closely with suppliers to achieve target cost objectives during the New Product Development Process.		0.5139
Factor C-2: SUPPLIERS IN A MAJOR NEW PRODUCT DEVELOPMENT ROLE	0.6922/ 10.2%	
12. When used, our suppliers play an important role in the design and development of new products.		0.7959
13. Suppliers are used frequently for New Product Development.		0.7569
14. When used, suppliers usually become involved in the New Product Development Process at the concept stage.		0.6152
Factor C-3: SUPPLIER INTEGRATION NEW PRODUCT DEVELOPMENT OUTCOMES	0.7503/ 8.9%	
27. Supplier integration into our New Product Development Process results in reduced time-to-market of new products.		0.8072
28. Supplier integration into our New Product Development Process results in higher product quality.		0.7644

---

[1]Jum C. Nunnally and Ira H. Bernstein, *Psychometric Theory,* 3rd edition (New York: McGraw-Hill, Inc., 1994), pp. 232-233.
[2]Factor Loadings are the correlations between each variable and each factor.

FACTOR ANALYSIS OF EARLY SUPPLIER INVOLVEMENT IN NEW PRODUCT
DEVELOPMENT QUESTIONNAIRE: SECTION C (CONTINUED)

Questionnaire Items	Reliability Coefficients (Alphas)[1]/ % of Variance	Factor Loadings[2]
Factor C-4: NEW PRODUCT DEVELOPMENT MUTUAL COMMITMENT	0.6287/ 6.6%	
18. Integration of a supplier into the New Product Development Process in our Business Unit happens only if that supplier's top management team is committed to their involvement.		0.5372
25. The commitment of our Business Unit's top management is needed to include a specific supplier in our New Product Development Process.		0.7510
26. There has to be a strong consensus within our Business Unit before a specific supplier is included in our New Product Development Process.		0.7243
Factor C-5: TIMING OF SUPPLIER NEW PRODUCT DEVELOPMENT INVOLVEMENT	0.7987/ 6.0%	
15. When used, suppliers usually become involved in the New Product Development Process after the concept has been finalized.		0.8295
16. When used, suppliers usually become involved in the New Product Development Process after the design has been finalized.		0.7530
Factor C-6: PROJECT TECHNOLOGICAL COMPLEXITY	0.2000 5.4%	
29. Suppliers are more likely to be integrated into New Product Development processes when the project is technologically complex.		0.8515
30. Suppliers share in cost savings they identify during the New Product Development Process.		

Total Variance Explained: 66.6%

Questionnaire Items Not Loading on Any Factor:

23. There must be a high level of familiarity with a supplier's capabilities before it is included in our Business Unit's New Product Development Process.

24. The New Product Development process in our Business Unit is very receptive to ideas that come from our suppliers.

---

[1]Jum C. Nunnally and Ira H. Bernstein, *Psychometric Theory,* 3rd edition (New York: McGraw-Hill, Inc., 1994), pp. 232-233.
[2]Factor Loadings are the correlations between each variable and each factor.

Exhibit A-4
FACTOR ANALYSIS OF EARLY SUPPLIER INVOLVEMENT IN NEW PRODUCT DEVELOPMENT QUESTIONNAIRE: SECTION D

Questionnaire Items	Reliability Coefficients (Alphas)[1]/ % of Variance	Factor Loadings[2]
Factor D-1: CONTINUING NEW PRODUCT DEVELOPMENT COMMITMENT	0.8038/ 42.4%	
34. Shared education and training programs between your Business Unit and suppliers.		0.5849
36. Co-location of Business Unit and supplier personnel.		0.7326
38. Training program in mutual trust development.		0.6863
41. Shared physical assets (plant and equipment) between suppliers and your Business Unit.		0.7299
42. Formalized risk/reward sharing agreements between your Business Unit and suppliers.		0.7215
Factor D-2: EXPLICIT NEW PRODUCT DEVELOPMENT PROCESSES	0.8408/ 10.1%	
32. Supplier membership/participation on your Business Unit's New Product Development project team.		0.5434
33. Direct cross-functional, intercompany communications between your Business Unit and suppliers.		0.7582
43. Joint agreement on performance measurements of the New Product Development Process.		0.5430
44. Business Unit cross-functional teams for supplier selection and planning.		0.8381
45. Formal processes for selecting suppliers to be integrated into the New Product Development process.		0.7700
Factor D-3: SHARING CONFIDENTIAL INFORMATION	0.7598/ 8.6%	
37. Frequent technology information sharing between your Business Unit and its suppliers on an "as-needed" basis.		0.6243
39. Sharing customer requirements with suppliers.		0.7829
40. Frequent and detailed sharing of product and process technology information between your Business Unit and its suppliers.		0.7947

Total Variance Explained: 61.1%

Questionnaire Item Not Loading On Any Factor:

35. Linked (EDI, CAD/CAM, e-mail) information systems.

---

[1]Jum C. Nunnally and Ira H. Bernstein, *Psychometric Theory,* 3rd edition (New York: McGraw-Hill, Inc., 1994), pp. 232-233.
[2]Factor Loadings are the correlations between each variable and each factor.

Exhibit A-5
FACTOR ANALYSIS OF EARLY SUPPLIER INVOLVEMENT IN NEW PRODUCT
DEVELOPMENT QUESTIONNAIRE: SECTION E

Questionnaire Items	Reliability Coefficients (Alphas)[1]/ % of Variance	Factor Loadings[2]
46. My Business Unit responds quickly and effectively to changing customer or supplier needs compared to our competition.		0.8753
47. My Business Unit responds quickly and effectively to changing competitor strategies compared to our competitors.		0.8842
48. My Business Unit develops and markets new products quickly and effectively compared to our competitors.		0.8336
49. In most of its markets my Business Unit is a very strong competitor.		0.7560
Factor E-2 COMPETITIVE HOSTILITY	0.7288/ 19.7%	
50. In the markets served by my Business Unit, the firm that eases up usually loses markets/customers to its competitors.		0.8463
51. Competition in the markets served by our Business Unit is severe.		0.8925

Total Variance Explained: 75.2%

---

[1]Jum C. Nunnally and Ira H. Bernstein, *Psychometric Theory,* 3rd edition (New York: McGraw-Hill, Inc., 1994), pp. 232-233.
[2]Factor Loadings are the correlations between each variable and each factor.

Exhibit A-6
EARLY SUPPLIER INVOLVEMENT IN NEW PRODUCT DEVELOPMENT
QUESTIONNAIRE: T-TEST OF STUDY FACTORS AND NEW PRODUCT SUCCESS

	Factors	Significance	New Product Success	
			High >3.26	Low <3.26
B-1	Purchasing in a Major New Product Development Role[1] 0.000	3.6842	3.0845	
B-2	New Product Success[1]	0.000	3.7289	2.7184
C-1	New Product Development Strategic Evaluation and Control[2]	0.000	3.8073	3.3262
C-2	Suppliers in a Major New Product Development Role[2]	0.080	3.8660	3.6810
C-3	Supplier Integration New Product Development Outcomes[2]	0.029	3.9433	3.7174
C-5	Timing of Supplier New Product Development Involvement[2]	0.249	2.7969	2.9565
D-1	Continuing New Product Development Commitment[3]	0.002	3.1958	2.6261
D-2	Explicit New Product Development Processes[3]	0.001	4.3553	3.7257
D-3	Sharing Confidential Information[3]	0.013	4.8125	4.3714
E-1	Business Unit Competitive Responsiveness[4]	0.000	3.9701	3.3523
E-2	Competitive Hostility[4]	0.001	4.1805	3.8259

[1]Means for these factors are based on the following scale: 1 = Strongly Disagree to 5 = Strongly Agree. Based on 250 of 252 respondents. High = 134, Low = 116.
[2]Scale: 1 = Strongly Disagree to 5 = Strongly Agree. Based on 167 of 168 respondents who indicated that suppliers participate in the New Product Development Process. High = 97, Low = 70.
[3]Scale: 1 = Never Used to 7 = Very Extensively Used. Based on 166 of 168 respondents who indicated that suppliers participate in the New Product Development Process. High = 96, Low = 70.
[4]Scale: 1 = Strongly Disagree to 5 = Strongly Agree. Based 246 of 252 respondents. High = 134, Low = 112.

Exhibit A-7
EARLY SUPPLIER INVOLVEMENT IN NEW PRODUCT DEVELOPMENT
QUESTIONNAIRE: T-TEST OF STUDY FACTORS AND SUPPLIER INVOLVEMENT

	Factors	Significance	Means[1] Supplier Participation in the New Product Development Process	
			Yes	No
B-1	Purchasing in a Major New Product Development Role[2]	0.000	3.6667	2.8795
B-2	New Product Success[2]	0.007	3.3413	3.0964
E-1	Business Unit Competitive Responsiveness[3]	0.305	3.7210	3.6080
E-2	Competitive Hostility	0.038	4.0884	3.8537

[1]Scale: 1 = Strongly Disagree to 5 = Strongly Agree.
[2]Based on all 252 respondents. Yes = 168, No = 84.
[3]Based on 246 of 252 respondents. Yes = 164, No = 82.

Exhibit A-8
REGRESSION ANALYSIS OF NEW PRODUCT SUCCESS

A. Based on 156 of 168 respondents who answered yes to the question "Do suppliers participate in the New Product Development Process in your Business Unit?

Dependent Variable:	B-2	New Product Success	
Independent Variables:	B-1	Purchasing in a Major New Product Development Role	
	C-1	New Product Development Strategic Evaluation and Control	
	C-3	Supplier Integration New Product Outcomes	
	D-1	Continuing New Product Development Commitment	
	D-2	Explicit New Product Development Processes	
	D-3	Sharing Confidential Information	
	E-1	Business Unit Competitive Responsiveness	
	E-2	Competitive Hostility	

	Coefficient of	Coefficients			
Step	Determination[1]	Constant	C-1	E-1	B-1
1	0.18048	1.840	0.419	-	-
2	0.24584	1.425	0.297	0.229	-
3	0.27572	1.208	0.219	0.208	0.157

B. Based on 80 of 84 respondents who answered no to the question "Do suppliers participate in the New Product Development Process in your Business Unit?

Dependent Variable:	B-2	New Product Success	
Independent Variables:	B-1	Purchasing in a Major New Product Development Role	
	E-1	Business Unit Competitive Responsiveness	
	E-2	Competitive Hostility	

	Coefficient of	Coefficients	
Step	Determination	Constant	E-1
1	0.35826	1.355	0.487

---

[1]The coefficient of determination, or r-square, reports the percent of variation in the dependent variable that is explained by the equation.

Exhibit A-9
EARLY SUPPLIER INVOLVEMENT IN NEW PRODUCT DEVELOPMENT
QUESTIONNAIRE: CONTINGENCY TABLE ANALYSIS OF SELECTED QUESTIONS
1. FOCUS ON NEW PRODUCT SUCCESS

A. New Product Success by Supplier Participation in New Product Development

Supplier Participation in New Product Development	Respondent Perceived New Product Success		
	High	Low	Total
Yes	97/ (89.5)[1]	70/ (77.5)	167
No	37/ (44.5)	46/ (38.5)	83
Total	134	116	250

Pearson Value = 4.0663, 1 degree of freedom
Significance = 0.0438
Missing Values = 2

B. New Product Success by Industry Category

Industrial Category	Respondent Perceived New Product Success		
	High	Low	Total
Manufacturing	91/ (90.3)	76/ (76.6)	167
Services	19/ (24.3)	26/ (20.7)	45
Other	23/ (18.4)	11/ (15.6)	34
Total	133	113	246

Pearson Value = 5.0790, 2 degrees of freedom
Significance = 0.0789
Missing Values = 6

C. New Product Success by Ownership of Business Unit

Ownership of Business Unit	Respondent Perceived New Product Success		
	High	Low	Total
United States	122/ (116.3)	93/ (98.7)	215
Other	10/ (15.7)	19/ (13.3)	29
Total	132	112	244

Pearson Value = 5.1000, 1 degree of freedom
Significance = 0.0239
Missing Values = 8

---

[1] Observed/ (Expected)

EARLY SUPPLIER INVOLVEMENT IN NEW PRODUCT DEVELOPMENT
QUESTIONNAIRE: CONTINGENCY TABLE ANALYSIS OF SELECTED QUESTIONS (CONTINUED)

1. FOCUS ON NEW PRODUCT SUCCESS (CONTINUED)

D. New Product Success by Years Experience in Purchasing

Years Experience in Purchasing	Respondent Perceived New Product Success		Total
	High	Low	Total
0 - 10	29/ (33.0)	32/ (28.0)	61
11 or more	105/ (101.0)	82/ (86.0)	187
Total	134	114	248

Pearson Value = 1.3724, 1 degree of freedom
Significance = 0.2414
Missing Values = 4

E. New Product Success by Professional Certification

Professional Certification	Respondent Perceived New Product Success		Total
	High	Low	Total
Yes	64/ (67.5)	62/ (58.5)	126
No	70/ (66.5)	54/ (57.5)	124
Total	136	116	250

Pearson Value = 0.8044, 1 degree of freedom
Significance = 0.3698
Missing Values = 2

EARLY SUPPLIER INVOLVEMENT IN NEW PRODUCT DEVELOPMENT
QUESTIONNAIRE: CONTINGENCY TABLE ANALYSIS OF SELECTED QUESTIONS (CONTINUED)

2. FOCUS ON SUPPLIER PARTICIPATION IN NEW PRODUCT DEVELOPMENT

A. Supplier Participation in New Product Development by Industry Category

Industry Category	Supplier Participation in New Product Development		Total
	Yes	No	
Manufacturing	130/ (111.8)	38/ (56.2)	168
Services	18/ (29.9)	27/ (15.1)	45
Other	17/ (23.3)	18/ (11.7)	35
Total	165	83	246

Pearson Value = 28.1171, 2 degrees of freedom
Significance = 0.0000
Missing Values = 4

B. Supplier Participation in New Product Development by Ownership of Business Unit

Ownership of Business Unit	Supplier Participation in New Product Development		Total
	Yes	No	
United States	142/ (144.7)	75/ (72.3)	217
Other	22/ (19.3)	7/ (9.7)	29
Total	164	82	246

Pearson Value = 1.2590, 1 degree of freedom
Significance = 0.2634
Missing Values = 6

EARLY SUPPLIER INVOLVEMENT IN NEW PRODUCT DEVELOPMENT
QUESTIONNAIRE: CONTINGENCY TABLE ANALYSIS OF SELECTED QUESTIONS (CONTINUED)

2. FOCUS ON SUPPLIER PARTICIPATION IN NEW PRODUCT DEVELOPMENT (CONTINUED)

C. Supplier Participation in New Product Development by Years of Experience in Purchasing

Years Experience in Purchasing	Supplier Participation in New Product Development		Total
	Yes	No	Total
0 - 10	32/ (41.4)	30 (20.6)	62
11 or more	135/ (125.6)	53/ (62.4)	188
Total	167	83	250

Pearson Value = 8.5745, 1 degree of freedom
Significance = 0.0034
Missing Values = 2

D. Supplier Participation in New Product Development by Professional Certification

Professional Certification?	Supplier Participation in New Product Development		Total
	Yes	No	Total
Yes	88/ (84.7)	39/ (42.3)	127
No Certifications	80/ (83.3)	45/ (41.7)	125
Total	168	84	252

Pearson Value = 0.7937, 1 degree of freedom
Significance = 0.3730
Missing Values = 0

EARLY SUPPLIER INVOLVEMENT IN NEW PRODUCT DEVELOPMENT
QUESTIONNAIRE: CONTINGENCY TABLE ANALYSIS OF SELECTED QUESTIONS (CONTINUED)

3. FOCUS ON INDUSTRY

A. Industry Category by Ownership of Business Unit

Ownership of Business Unit	Industry Category			
	Manufacturing	Services	Other	Total
United States	139/ (146.4)	44/ (39.7)	34/ (30.9)	217
Other	27/ (19.6)	1/ (5.3)	1/ (4.1)	29
Total	166	45	35	246

Pearson Value = 9.8439, 2 degrees of freedom
Significance = 0.0073
Missing Values = 6

B. Industry Category by Years Experience in Purchasing

Years Experience in Purchasing	Industry Category			
	Manufacturing	Services	Other	Total
0 - 10	41/ (42.1)	11/ (11.1)	10/ (8.8)	62
11 or more	126/ (124.9)	33/ (32.9)	25/ (26.2)	184
Total	167	44	35	246

Pearson Value = 0.2493, 2 degrees of freedom
Significance = 0.8828
Missing Values = 6

C. Industry Category by Professional Certification

Professional Certification	Industry Category			
	Manufacturing	Services	Other	Total
Certified Purchasing Manager	40 (37.9)	7 (10.2)	9 (7.9)	56
Other Certifications	52 (46.7)	9 (12.5)	8 (9.7)	69
No Certifications	76 (83.3)	29 (22.3)	18 (17.4)	123
Total	168	45	35	248

Pearson Value = 5.8069, 4 degrees of freedom
Significance = 0.2140
Missing Values = 4

APPENDIX IV: STUDY B: PURCHASING AND SUPPLIER INVOLVEMENT IN PRODUCTION PROCESS DEVELOPMENT AND IMPROVEMENT •

METHODOLOGY AND RESULTS

Methodology

The methodology section describes the techniques used to gather the data used in the study. It provides a means for the technically inclined reader to evaluate the research techniques used.

Questionnaire Development

A five page, 48-item questionnaire was developed to gather data regarding the importance of process to the business unit, purchasing's role in process development and improvement, the supplier's role in process development and improvement, the competitive environment, and general information. "Process" is defined as any production/operations process that uses materials and supplies, capital equipment, labor, and information to convert inputs into products/services. "Process Development/Improvement" is defined as procedures that guide the conceptualization, design, engineering, manufacturing, and implementation of changes to production/operations processes.

The questionnaire focused on 11 research issues. Ten of these issues were developed from the research issues addressed in the "Early Supplier Involvement in New Product Development" questionnaire and from a review of the limited literature that addresses process development*. One issue gathered information about the respondents. The classification of questionnaire items relevant to the research issues was as follows:

RESEARCH ISSUE	NUMBER OF QUESTIONNAIRE ITEMS
1. Supplier Involvement in Process Development/Improvement	2
2. Role of Purchasing	6
3. Supplier Identification/Certification	4
4. Timing of Involvement	6
5. Technology Sharing	1
6. Monitoring and Control	6
7. Risk/Rewards	1
8. Time/Quality/Cost Savings	5
9. Importance of Process Development/Improvement Relative to New Product Development	1
10. The Business Unit and Its Market	14
11. Respondent Information	2

The questionnaire was organized into five sections: Focus of the Questionnaire (Section A), Processes in Your Business Unit (Section B), Purchasing's Role in New Process Development/Improvement (Section C), The Supplier's Role in Process Development/Improvement (Section D), Competitive Environment (Section E), and General Information (Section F). The questionnaire, prenotification letter, cover letter, and follow-up letter are shown in the Appendix II.

Sampling and Response Analysis

A random sample of 1,074 National Association of Purchasing Management (NAPM) members in NAPM's "Title 1" (purchasing senior management) category was selected from the 50 United States. A prenotification letter was mailed to each individual one week prior to mailing the questionnaire and cover letter. A follow-up letter was sent to each individual one week later.

By the cut-off date for responses, 271 usable responses had been received. The usable response rate of 25.2

---

* Please see annotated bibliography.

PURCHASING INVOLVEMENT IN PRODUCTION PROCESS DEVELOPMENT QUESTIONNAIRE
RESPONSE RATES

Industry Category	Population Number/ Percentage	Estimated Number in Sample[1]	Usable Responses/ Usable Response Percent of Estimated Sample	Percentage of Total Respondents
Manufacturing	1274/36.5%	392	169/43.1%	62.4%
Service	804/23.0%	247	47/19.0%	17.3%
Other	1417/40.5%	435	55/12.6%	20.3%
Missing Values	0	0	0	0
Totals	3,495/100%	1,074/100%	271/25.2%	100%

[1]Estimated Number in the Sample = [(Number in the Population)/3,495] x [1,074]

percent was deemed adequate for analysis. Analysis of the respondents by industry category indicated the estimated response rate for manufacturing firms was 43.1 percent, service firms 19.0 percent, and other 12.6 percent. The composition of all respondents was 62.4 percent from manufacturing, 17.3 percent from services, and 20.3 percent from other industry categories. Exhibit B-1 summarizes the questionnaire response rate.

Analysis of the usable responses by ZIP Code, as determined by the postmark on the business reply envelope or the respondents' request for a summary of the results, indicated that the response rate by geographical region did not differ by an amount greater than that due to chance.

Overall, the respondents reflected the geographical distribution of the sample, and were more representative of manufacturing and less representative of other industry categories.

DATA ANALYSIS

The data analysis section provides the technically inclined reader with the opportunity to examine the techniques used to arrive at the results reported in the study.

Factor Analysis

Factor Analysis is a data reduction technique that enables the researcher to identify underlying ideas or constructs contained in a series of questionnaire items. This enables the researcher to (a) simplify a large number of questionnaire items into a smaller number of constructs and (b) identify specific questionnaire items that explicitly describe complex constructs.

The authors felt this technique would be useful because of the limitations of describing data that includes a large number of variables.

Two issues are relevant in this type of analysis. First, do the factors identified make sense? The questions associated with a factor have to make sense if they are to be useful for further analysis. For example, a factor that included apples, oranges, and grapes might be considered "fruit." However, a factor that included apples, fish, and limestone might not make sense for purposes of further analysis. The issue that addresses "Does the factor make sense?" is *validity*. Validity is concerned with how well the factor (or any social science measuring instrument) measures the concept identified in the factor analysis. The issue of validity will be addressed as each factor is discussed.

Second, is the statistical reliability of the factors adequate for further analysis? *Reliability* refers to the internal consistency among (or between) the variables in a factor. Factors with high reliability are more likely to be reproducible in subsequent studies. The measure of reliability used in this research is the reliability coefficient, commonly referred to as the Cronbach's coefficient alpha. In this research, an alpha of 0.70 or greater was considered adequate.

Generally, a factor must make sense (be valid) and have adequate reliability to be useful for purposes of analysis. One factor in the absence of the other does not result in a useful factor.

The statistical package used in this study was **SPSS for Microsoft Windows 6.2.** Principal Components was used with a limiting Eigenvalue of 1.0 or greater for Varimax Rotation. These options maximize internal similarity of factors and minimize the similarity among (or between) factors.

Factor Analysis of the Purchasing Involvement in Production Process Development and Improvement Questionnaire, Section B.

As shown in Exhibit B-2, one factor was identified in Section B. This factor consists of five questionnaire items. These questions address the importance of process to the business unit in terms of cost and quality advantage, achieving time-to-market schedules, and priority. Examination of the five questions resulted in the name *Process as a Source of Competitive Advantage.* The reliability coefficient of 0.7764 was above the value of 0.70 thought to be adequate for basic research. It was concluded that face validity and reliability of this factor was adequate for use in subsequent analysis.

The second factor was composed of two questionnaire items that related to process development and improvement relative to new product development and whether purchasing has the necessary skills and knowledge to contribute effectively to process development/ improvement. Because the reliability of this difficult-to-interpret factor was 0.4036, it was decided not to use this factor in subsequent analysis.

Factor Analysis of the Purchasing Involvement in Production Process Development and Improvement Questionnaire, Section C.

As shown in Exhibit B-3, one interpretable factor was identified in Section C. This factor comprised six questionnaire items that addressed purchasing's role in process development and improvement in the areas of constant involvement, roles in cross-functional teams, and identifying technology and suppliers that are important to process development and improvement. This factor was named *Purchasing in a Major Process Development/Improvement Role.*

The reliability coefficient of this factor was 0.8617, well above the value of 0.70 thought to be adequate for basic research. It was concluded that face validity and reliability of *Purchasing in a Major Process Development/ Improvement Role* was adequate for use in subsequent analysis.

Factor Analysis of the Purchasing Involvement in Production Process Development and Improvement Questionnaire, Section D.

As shown in Exhibit B-4, four interpretable factors were identified. The first factor, *Supplier Integration Outcomes in Process Development/Improvement,* consisted of four questionnaire items that addressed supplier contributions to reduced time-to-market and higher product quality, supplier sharing of cost savings, and buyer-supplier cooperation to achieve target costs. The reliability coefficient (alpha) for this factor was 0.7196. The second factor, *Openness to Supplier Involvement in Process Development/Improvement,* comprised four items. These items focus on frequent, close coordination in which the buying organization is receptive to supplier ideas. This factor's alpha was 0.7171.

Process Improvement Strategic Evaluation (alpha = 0.8273) was composed of two questions that focus on the respondent's organization carefully evaluating whether process technology and quality objectives are better met internally or by a supplier. The fourth factor, *Timing of Supplier Involvement in Development/ Improvement,* contained two items. These items focused on purchasing becoming involved in process development/improvement late in the process. The alpha for this factor was 0.7546.

Three factors did not meet the authors validity or reliability criteria and were not used in subsequent analysis.

Factor Analysis of the Purchasing Involvement in Production Process Development and Improvement Questionnaire, Section E.

Questionnaire items 37 through 42 were based on two scales used previously for logistics strategy research. The two resulting factors were similar to the previously used scales. *Business Unit Competitive Responsiveness* (reliability coefficient = 0.7583) comprised three of the four items usually associated with that scale. These three items focused on the business unit's ability to respond to customer and supplier changing needs, responding to competitor strategies, and developing new products quickly and effectively. Three, rather than two items, loaded on *Competitive Hostility.* The reliability coefficient was 0.6240. This analysis is shown as Exhibit B-5.

Factor Analysis, Development of Factor Scores

The development of factor scores for each respondent provides a means by which the relevance of the factors can be related to the research objectives.

Factor scores were calculated for each individual respondent on each of the 11 factors that met the authors' validity and reliability objectives. The factor score is the arithmetic average of all questionnaire items loading on the factor. For example, the factor score for each individual on Factor B-1 would be the sum of that respondent's responses to questionnaire items 1, 2, 3, 4, and 5 divided by five.

Respondent factor scores can be used to divide respondents into "high" and "low" categories based on their scores, to compare respondent mean scores between two or more categories, or statistically compare relationships among two or more factors.

In the next section, the t-test is used to compare individual factor scores between levels of product success, between respondents who include suppliers in new product development, and between respondents who consider their business units to be *high* on competitive responsiveness and those who are *low* on competitive responsiveness. Finally, the t-test was used to ascertain whether any of the factors differed with business unit size in terms of employment or sales.

T-Tests of Selected Variables

The t-test is a statistical test between the means of two samples. The purpose of this test is to determine if the two means differ by an amount greater than that due to chance. For example, if the means of A and B are significantly different at the 0.05 level, it can be concluded that the difference is not merely due to chance variation in the data. Conversely, if the pair is not significantly different at the 0.05 level, it would be concluded that the differences in means are due to chance variations in the data.

In the second stage of the analysis respondent factor scores on selected factors were divided into "high" and "low" categories. The statistical t-test was then conducted between *high* and *low* categories to ascertain statistical differences between categories and respondent factor scores. The purpose of this analysis was to provide the researchers with insights into factors that might be managerially useful in managing early supplier involvement in production process development and improvement. The following paragraphs present these results.

T-test of Process as a Source of Competitive Advantage With Selected Factors

Respondents were divided into "high" and "low" categories based on their *Process as a Source of Competitive Advantage* factor scores. Seven of eight factors were significant at the 0.05 level of significance. These results provide insights into which factors are likely to contribute to successful process development and improvement.

As shown in Exhibit B-6, respondents with *high* factor scores were compared to respondent with *low* factor

scores on Factor B-1: Process as a Source of Competitive Advantage. Seven factors were significant:

C-1: Purchasing in a Major Process Development/ Improvement Role
D-1: Supplier Integration in Process Development/ Improvement Outcomes
D-2: Openness to Supplier Involvement in Process Development/Improvement
D-3: Process Development/Improvement Strategic Evaluation
E-1: Business Unit Competitive Responsiveness
E-2: Competitive Hostility

Respondent factor scores for one factor did not differ significantly at the 0.05 level:

D-5: Timing of Supplier Involvement in Process Development/Improvement

Respondents who consider their business units to be above average on process as a source of competitive advantage were more likely to perceive that:

1. Purchasing plays a major role in process improvement/development, including constant involvement, playing important roles in process improvement/ development cross-functional teams, and in identifying technology and suppliers that are important to process development/improvement.

2. Supplier integration into process development/ improvement results in reduced product time-to-market and higher product quality, supplier identified cost savings are shared, and the business unit works closely with suppliers to achieve target cost objectives.

3. Supplier efforts are used frequently and are closely coordinated, and that those responsible for process development/improvement are very receptive to supplier ideas.

4. Their business unit carefully evaluates whether new process technology and quality objectives are better met within the business unit or by suppliers.

5. Their business unit is a strong competitor by being more responsive to changing customer needs, supplier needs, and competitor strategies.

6. Their business unit is a strong competitor in a hostile market.

Respondents who consider their business units to be above average on process as a source of competitive advantage were no different from respondents who were below average, in the following area:

1. Suppliers become involved in process improvement/development after the concept has been finalized.

T-test of Purchasing's Participation in Process Development/Improvement With Selected Factors

Respondents were divided into two categories based on their response to question 9: "Does purchasing participate in new process development/improvement in your business unit?" Four of eight factors were significant at the 0.05 level of significance. These results provide insights into which factors are likely to be associated with purchasing's involvement in process development/improvement.

As shown in Exhibit B-7, four of seven factors were significant at the 0.05 level:

B-1: Process as a Source of Competitive Advantage
D-1: Supplier Integration in Process Development/Improvement Outcomes
D-2: Openness to Supplier Involvement in Process Development/Improvement
D-5: Timing of Supplier Involvement in Process Development/Improvement

The following respondent factor scores did not differ significantly at the 0.05 level:

D-3: Process Improvement Strategic Evaluation
E-1: Business Unit Competitive Responsiveness
E-2: Competitive Hostility

Respondents whose business unit's purchasing department is involved in process development and improvement were more likely to perceive that:

1. Processes are a source of cost and quality advantage, contribute to product time-to-market schedules, and are high priority.

2. Supplier integration into process development/improvement results in reduced product time-to-market and higher product quality, supplier identified cost savings are shared, and the business unit works closely with suppliers to achieve target cost objectives.

3. Supplier efforts are used frequently and are closely coordinated, and those responsible for process development/improvement are very receptive to supplier ideas.

4. Suppliers become involved in process improvement/development before the concept has been finalized.

Factor scores of respondents whose business unit's purchasing department is involved in process development did not differ at the 0.05 level from those who are not involved, in the following areas:

1. Their business unit carefully evaluates whether new process technology and quality objectives are better met within the business unit or by suppliers.

2. More likely to perceive their business unit as a very strong competitor by being more responsive to changing customer needs, supplier needs, and competitor strategies.

3. More likely to perceive their business unit as being a strong competitor in a hostile market.

T-test of Supplier Participation in Process Development/Improvement With Selected Factors

Respondents were divided into two categories based on their response to question 17: "Do suppliers participate in new process development/improvement in your business unit?" Two of four factors were significant at the 0.05 level of significance. These results provide insights into which factors are likely to be associated with supplier involvement in process development/improvement.

As shown in Exhibit B-8, two of four factors were significant at the 0.05 level:

B-1: Process as a Source of Competitive Advantage
C-1: Purchasing in a Major Process Development/Improvement Role

The following respondent factor scores did not differ significantly at the 0.05 level:

E-1: Business Unit Competitive Responsiveness
E-2: Competitive Hostility

Respondents whose business unit involved suppliers in process development and improvement are more likely to perceive that:

1. Processes are a source of cost and quality advantage, contribute to product time-to-market schedules, and are high priority.

2. Purchasing plays a major role in process improvement/development, is involved constantly, plays important roles in process improvement/development cross-functional teams, and identifies technology and suppliers that are important to process development/improvement.

Factor scores of respondents whose suppliers are involved in process development did not differ at the 0.05 level from those whose suppliers were not involved, in the following areas:

1. More likely to perceive their business unit as a very strong competitor by being more responsive to changing customer needs, supplier needs, and competitor strategies.

2. More likely to perceive their business unit as being a strong competitor in a hostile market.

T-test of Factor Scores With Business Unit Employment and Sales

This test was performed to ascertain whether organizational size affected respondent perceptions.

Based on individual factor scores, the respondents were divided into *High* and *Low* categories on each of the eight factors. The questionnaire means of items 44a (Number of employees employed by your business unit) and 45 (Approximate annual sales of your business unit last year) for the *high* and *low* categories of each factor were compared using the t-test.

Of the 16 comparisons, one was significant at the 0.05 level. *Number of Employees* averaged 2,709 in business units in the *high* category of factor D-5: Timing of Supplier Involvement in Process Development/Improvement. The average number of employees in the *low* category was 5,148. None of the other 15 comparisons was significant at the 0.05 level. It was concluded that business unit size, in terms of employment or annual revenue, does not substantially affect overall purchasing and supplier involvement in process development and improvement.

Contingency Table Analysis with the Chi-square Statistic of Selected Variables

Contingency table analysis with the chi-square test is used when the variables being analyzed are nominal. For example, comparing respondents classified as *high* and *low* on dimension A and *high* and *low* on dimension B would be an appropriate use of the contingency table analysis. The t-test would not be appropriate in this example because neither of the variables are interval.

In this step of the analysis, the statistical relationships among six nominally scaled variables were evaluated using contingency table analysis with the chi-square statistic. This technique is the nonparametric test for use with nominally scaled data. Interpretation of the results is similar to the t-test. If the observed results differ from the expected results at the 0.05 level, it can be concluded that the differences are greater than what would be

expected due to chance. If the results are not significant at the 0.05 level, it would be concluded that differences between observed and expected results do not differ by an amount greater than that due to chance. The seven variables analyzed in this step of the analysis were:

1. Process as a Source of Competitive Advantage (High, Low)
2. Purchasing Participation in Process Development/ Improvement (Yes, No)
3. Supplier Participation in Process Development/ Improvement (Yes, No)
4. Industry Category (Manufacturing, Services, Other)
5. Ownership of Business Unit (United States, Other)
6. Respondent Years of Experience in Purchasing (0-10 Years, 11 Years of More)
7. Professional Certification (One or more professional certifications, No Certification)

Contingency Table Analysis of Process as a Source of Competitive Advantage With Selected Variables

Respondents were divided into high and low categories based on their *Process as a Source of Competitive Advantage* factor scores. Three of six variables (Purchasing Participation in Process Improvement/ Development, Supplier Participation in Process Improvement/ Development, and Industry Category) were not independent of *Process as a Source of Competitive Advantage*. Three variables (Ownership of the Business Unit, Years of Experience in Purchasing, and Professional Certification) were independent of *Process as a Source of Competitive Advantage*.

Respondents whose business units were *high* on *Process as a Source of Competitive Advantage* were:

1. More likely to have purchasing involved in process development/improvement.

2. More likely to have suppliers involved in process development/improvement.

3. More likely to be manufacturing firms, rather than firms in the service or other industry categories.

Three variables were independent of *Process as a Source of Competitive Advantage:* ownership of the business unit, years experience in purchasing, and professional certification.

Contingency Table Analysis of Purchasing Participation in Process Development/ Improvement With Selected Variables

Respondents were divided into two categories based on their response to questionnaire item 9: "Does purchasing participate in process development/ improvement?" As shown in Exhibit B-9, three variables were not independent of *Purchasing Participation in New Process Development/Improvement*. Respondents whose business units participate in process development/improvement were:

1. More likely to have suppliers involved in process development/improvement.

2. More likely to be in manufacturing firms or service firms, rather than other industry categories.

3. More likely to have 0-10 years experience in purchasing.

Two variables were independent of *Purchasing Participation in Process Development/Improvement*. Respondents whose business units participate in process development/improvement were not significantly different from respondents whose business units do not participate in process development/improvement on:

1. Business Ownership (U.S. or other)

2. Professional Certification

Contingency Table Analysis of Supplier Participation in Process Development/Improvement With Selected Variables

Respondents were divided into two categories based on their response to questionnaire item 17: "Do suppliers participate in new process development/ improvement?" As shown in Exhibit B-9, one variable was not independent of *Supplier Participation in New Process Development/Improvement*. Respondents whose business units include suppliers in process development/improvement were:

1. More likely to be manufacturing firms, rather than service or other industry categories.

Three variables were independent of *Supplier Participation in Process Development/Improvement*. Respondents whose business units include suppliers in process development/improvement were not significantly different from respondents whose business units do not include suppliers in process development/improvement on:

1. Business Ownership (U.S. or other)

2. Years Experience in Purchasing

3. Professional Certification

DISCUSSION

This portion of the report interprets the research results and discusses their implications.

Insights from the Factor Analysis

Factor B-1: Process as a Source of Competitive Advantage

A commonly accepted understanding is that competitive advantage can be achieved in three ways through: (a) cost advantage, (b) meaningful differentiation, and (c) a combination of cost advantage and meaningful differentiation. Process development and improvement can contribute to both. For example, a process improvement that simultaneously reduces cost, improves quality, and reduces set-up time would provide competitive advantages in both dimensions.

The questions loading on Factor B-1 address the issues of competitive advantage well. It is important to note that the five questionnaire items loading on this factor are not independent. Rather, the perception of process as a source of competitive advantage is a composite of cost, quality, and time-to-market advantage and its priority in the business unit.

Managers thinking of processes as a source of competitive advantage should keep in mind that there are multiple facets involved. For example, focusing on only cost improvement, or only quality, or only new product time-to-market will probably result in minimal, or no, competitive advantage.

Factor C-1: Purchasing in a Major Process Development/Improvement Role

According to Factor C-1, purchasing plays three roles in process development and improvement: (a) constant involvement, (b) taking a positive leadership role in cross-functional teams, and (c) technology and supplier identification. While it is possible for purchasing to contribute to process development/improvement without playing all three roles, the results indicate that it is unlikely for purchasing to play a important part if it does not participate meaningfully in all three roles.

The key to purchasing's ability to contribute to process development/improvement is its role in cross-functional teams. This role provides the opportunity for purchasing to gather, translate, and disseminate information among a diverse array of internal customers, functions, suppliers, and potential suppliers. This role is consistent with the concept of total quality management (continuous improvement and the elimination of waste) currently fashionable in the trade press. The constant interaction among purchasing and the other participants should enable the business unit to constantly improve its processes over time.

Purchasing managers who want to maximize their department's contribution to competitive advantage in the area of process development and improvement may make progress toward that goal through a strategy of continuous interest, willingness to participate in cross-functional teams, and constant monitoring of current and prospective suppliers to identify potentially applicable technology.

Factor D-1: Supplier Integration in Process Development/Improvement Outcomes

According to the results, the outcomes of supplier integration in process development/improvement are measurable contributions to competitive advantage in terms of reduced new product time-to-market, higher product quality, shared cost savings, and the achievement of target-cost objectives. Questions loading on this factor address competitive advantage outcomes very well.

This factor provides purchasing managers with measurable dimensions that may be helpful in establishing objectives and evaluating outcomes of process development/improvement programs. For example, such a program might include specific goals in terms of reduced time-to-market, quality improvement, cost savings, and target costs.

Factor D-2: Openness to Supplier Involvement in Process Development/Improvement

This factor provides a basis for evaluating the openness of a business unit to supplier involvement in process development/improvement. In particular, this factor may be useful for evaluating multiple organizations. In an individual business unit, the items loading on this factor provide a frame of reference that may be useful for evaluating receptiveness to supplier involvement. For example, an audit of a business unit's receptiveness to supplier participation in process development/improvement could address the three issues of (a) frequency of supplier use, (b) closeness of coordination, and (c) receptiveness to supplier ideas. High evaluations on those three dimensions would suggest openness, while low evaluations would suggest a low level of receptiveness.

Factor D-3: Process Development/Improvement Strategic Evaluation

This factor provides a reference for the level of consideration that goes into the decision of whether or not to use suppliers in process development/improvement programs. Qualitative and quantitative evaluation techniques could be used to specifically decide whether or not to use suppliers.

Factor D-5: The Timing of Supplier Involvement in Process Development/ Improvement

This factor provides an indication of when suppliers are used in process development/improvement. Because of the wording of the questions in this factor, a *high* factor score would indicate later supplier involvement and a *low* factor score would indicate earlier supplier involvement.

Factor E-1: Business Unit Competitive Responsiveness

This factor represents a scale similar to one that has been used several times in logistics strategy research. It evaluates the business unit in terms of time responsiveness. Such a scale could be useful in evaluating the ability of a business unit to compete on the basis of time.

Factor E-2: Competitive Hostility

This factor represents a scale similar to one used several times in logistics research to evaluate the severity of market competition. In this questionnaire, the reliability coefficient was below 0.70. However, this factor was included in the analysis because a similar factor was used in the analysis of the New Product Development study.

T-Tests of Selected Variables

T-test of Process as a Source of Competitive Advantage With Selected Factors

Business units that perceive process as a source of competitive advantage are more likely to have purchasing departments that:
- are more involved in process development/ improvement
- carefully evaluate whether suppliers should be involved in process development/improvement programs
- use suppliers earlier, more frequently and effectively, with better coordination; and achieve better perceived results

Finally, business units that perceive process as a source of competitive advantage are more likely to be time competitive and perceive their competitive environment as hostile.

The results of this analysis, as shown in Exhibit B-6, indicate that six variables are associated with process as a source of competitive advantage. According to these results, business units that are above average in process as a source of competitive advantage are likely to have purchasing play a major role in process development/ improvement.

If suppliers participate in process development/improvement, business units that are above average in perceiving process as a source of competitive advantage are more likely to (a) obtain better outcomes from suppliers in terms of reduced time-to-market of new products, higher product quality, and closer cooperation in working to achieve target cost objectives, (b) are more likely to work closely with those suppliers, and be receptive to their ideas, (c) are more likely to evaluate whether process technology and quality objectives are better developed by suppliers, and (d) more likely to involve suppliers earlier in process development/improvement programs.

Business units that are above average in perceived importance of process as a source of competitive advantage are more likely to be time competitive and to perceive their competitive environments as being hostile.

T-test of Purchasing's Participation in Process Development/Improvement With Selected Factors

As shown in Exhibit B-7, 222 of 271 respondents (81.9%) indicated that purchasing participates in process development/improvement. These results also indicate that supplier participation in process development/improvement is associated with a higher level of perceived importance of process as a source of competitive advantage, as discussed in the previous section.

If suppliers participate in process development/improvement, business units whose purchasing departments participate are more likely to (a) obtain better outcomes from suppliers in terms of reduced time-to-market of new products, higher product quality, and closer cooperation in working to achieve target cost objectives, (b) work closely with those suppliers and be receptive to their ideas, and (c) more likely to involve suppliers earlier in process development/improvement programs.

Purchasing participation in process development/improvement was independent of business unit competitive responsiveness and competitive hostility.

T-test of Supplier Participation in Process Development/Improvement With Selected Factors

As shown in Exhibit B-8, 203 of 271 respondents indicated that suppliers participate in process development/improvement in their business unit. These results also indicate that supplier participation in process development/improvement is associated with (a) a perceived increase in the importance of process as a source of competitive advantage in the business unit and (b) purchasing is more likely to be perceived as playing a major role in process development/improvement. Supplier participation in process development/improvement was indepen-

dent of business unit competitive responsiveness and competitive hostility.

Contingency Table Analysis With the Chi-square Statistic of Selected Variables

Contingency Table Analysis of Process as a Source of Competitive Advantage With Selected Variables

Contingency table analysis with the chi-square statistic was conducted to (a) further examine the relationships of process as a source of competitive advantage with purchasing and supplier participation in process development/improvement and (b) examine the relationship of process as a source of competitive advantage with industry category, business unit ownership, respondent experience, and respondent professional certification.

According to Table 1A of Exhibit B-9, 149 out of 266 of the respondents perceived process as a source of competitive advantage to be *high* (56.0%), while 136 out of 219 of the respondents whose purchasing department participates, were in the *high* category (62.1%). Only 13 out of 47 whose purchasing department does not participate were in the high category (27.7%). As shown in Table 1B the results were similar for supplier participation in process development/improvement. The overall results, 149 out of 266 (56.0%) were the same as before. A total of 131 out of 199 (65.8%) of the respondents who reported that suppliers participated in process development/improvement perceived process as a source of competitive advantage to be *high,* while only 18 out of 67 (26.9%) of the respondents who reported that suppliers did not participate were *high.*

These results confirmed the findings in the earlier t-tests. However, the percentage participation provides additional insight into the importance the perception of process as a source of competitive advantage to expanded purchasing and supplier roles in process development/improvement.

According to Table 1C of Exhibit B-9, manufacturing firms were more likely to consider process to be a source of competitive advantage, 104 out of 164 (61.9%), than the respondents overall, 149 out of 266 (56.0%). Similar numbers for the service and "other" industries, 45 out of 98 (45.9%) revealed that process is less likely to be a source of competitive advantage outside of manufacturing. Two perspectives can explain these results:

1. There is greater potential for processes to contribute to competitive advantage in manufacturing industries, or
2. "Service" and "Other" industry categories have not yet exploited processes as a source of competitive advantage.

While the former perspective may have merit, the authors believe there is a reservoir of unrealized potential in the service and other industry categories for realization of process as a source of competitive advantage. A sizable minority, 45.9 percent, of respondents outside of manufacturing considered process as a source of competitive advantage to be *high*. Purchasing professionals and general management outside of manufacturing should closely examine the role processes play in delivering value. The authors believe an examination of this issue will result in the increased importance of process outside of manufacturing.

Three issues were independent of process as a source of competitive advantage, according to Tables 1D, 1E, and 1F of Exhibit B-9. Table 1D indicates that nation of ownership does not affect the perception of process as a source of competitive advantage. Apparently, nation of ownership plays no significant role in terms of recognition of process as a source of competitive advantage. Examination of Tables E and F revealed that experience in purchasing and professional certification were independent of process as a source of competitive advantage.

Contingency Table Analysis of Purchasing Participation in Process Development/Improvement With Selected Variables

Examination of Table 2A of Exhibit B-9 indicated that supplier participation in process development/improvement was greater when purchasing participates. A total of 177 out of 203 (87.2%) of those respondents who stated that purchasing participated in process development/improvement also reported that suppliers participated, while 222 out of 271 (82.2%) of the respondents overall reported that suppliers participate.

Purchasing participation in process development/improvement was significant, as shown in Table 2B. Further examination of the results indicated that purchasing participation did not differ significantly between "manufacturing" and "service" industry categories. The "other" industry category was lower. These results are interesting because service seems to lag behind manufacturing on most measures of process involvement.

Table 2C of Exhibit B-9 indicates purchasing is more likely to be involved in process development/improvement when the respondent has less experience in purchasing. Possibly, purchasing executives who have moved into the department from other areas of the firm may be more receptive to, or better able to facilitate, purchasing's participation.

Both business unit ownership and respondent professional certification were independent of purchasing participation in process development/improvement.

Contingency Table Analysis of Purchasing Participation in Process Development/Improvement With Selected Variables

Manufacturing business unit suppliers were more likely to participate in process development/improvement, according to Table 3A of Exhibit B-9. Results showed 135 out of 169 (79.9%) of the respondents from the manufacturing category reported supplier participation, while 68 out of 102 (66.7%) of the respondents in the service and other industry category reported supplier participation.

Business unit ownership, years experience in purchasing, and professional certification were independent of supplier involvement.

Overall Insights From the Contingency Table Analysis

The contingency table analysis highlights the interdependency of process as a source of competitive advantage, purchasing participation in process development/improvement, and supplier participation in process development/improvement. In addition, these three issues vary with industry category. While firms in manufacturing, service, and "other" industry categories emphasize process as a source of competitive advantage, purchasing participation, and supplier participation, the emphasis in manufacturing is greater.

That business unit ownership was independent of process, purchasing participation, and supplier participation suggests that U.S. purchasing department perceptions are independent of nation of ownership. With one exception, experience and professional certification were independent. The exception is that purchasing executives with 10 years experience or less are more likely to report that purchasing participates in process development/improvement.

Purchasing executives in industry categories other than manufacturing should not assume that process cannot be a source of competitive advantage in their firms, and that purchasing and suppliers cannot contribute to this source of competitive advantage. Rather, the results suggest the potential for purchasing and supplier contributions to the competitive advantage potential of process development/improvement is genuine.

Exhibit B-2
FACTOR ANALYSIS OF PURCHASING INVOLVEMENT IN PRODUCTION PROCESS
DEVELOPMENT AND IMPROVEMENT QUESTIONNAIRE: SECTION B

Questionnaire Items	Reliability Coefficients (Alphas)[1]/ % of Variance	Factor Loadings[2]
Factor B-1: PROCESS AS A SOURCE OF COMPETITIVE ADVANTAGE	0.7764/ 36.9%	
1. In my Business Unit, processes are a source of cost advantage.		0.7087
2. In my Business Unit, processes are a source of quality advantage.		0.7826
3. The processes of my Business Unit contribute to meeting or beating new product time-to-market schedules.		0.7340
4. Process Development/Improvement is a high priority in my Business Unit.		0.7198
5. Process Development/Improvement is a high priority in my Business Unit for existing products.		0.6110
Factor B-2: PROCESS DEVELOPMENT PRIORITY/ PURCHASING SKILLS/ KNOWLEDGE	0.4036/ 16.1%	
7. In my Business Unit, Process Development/Improvement is more important than New Product Development.		0.8315
8. In my Business Unit, purchasing has the skills and knowledge to contribute effectively to process development/improvement.		0.6536

Total Variance Explained: 53.0%

Questionnaire Item Not Loading on Any Factor:

6. Those responsible for Process Development/Improvement in my
    Business Unit have a "not invented here" mentality.

---

[1]Jum C. Nunnally and Ira H. Bernstein, *Psychometric Theory,* 3rd edition (New York: McGraw-Hill, Inc., 1994), pp. 232-233.
[2]Factor Loadings are the correlations between each variable and each factor.

FACTOR ANALYSIS OF PURCHASING INVOLVEMENT IN PRODUCTION PROCESS
DEVELOPMENT AND IMPROVEMENT QUESTIONNAIRE: SECTION C

Questionnaire Items	Reliability Coefficients (Alphas)[1]/ % of Variance	Factor Loadings[2]
Factor C-1: PURCHASING IN A MAJOR PROCESS DEVELOPMENT/IMPROVEMENT ROLE	0.8617/ 56.7%	
10. Purchasing plays a major role in Process Development/Improvement.		0.8332
11. Purchasing is constantly involved in Process Development/Improvement.		0.7847
13. Purchasing plays an important role in Process Development/Improvement cross-functional teams.		0.7578
14. Purchasing takes a leadership role in Process Development/Improvement cross-functional teams.		0.7878
15. Purchasing plays an important role in identifying technology that is important to Process Development/Improvement.		0.7215
16. Purchasing plays an important role in identifying suppliers that are important to Process Development/Improvement.		0.6889

Total Variance Explained: 56.7%

Questionnaire Item Not Loading on Any Factor:

12. Purchasing becomes involved in Process Development/Improvement only after most of the design decisions have been finalized.

[1]Jum C. Nunnally and Ira H. Bernstein, *Psychometric Theory,* 3rd edition (New York: McGraw-Hill, Inc., 1994), pp. 232-233.
[2]Factor Loadings are the correlations between each variable and each factor.

FACTOR ANALYSIS OF PURCHASING INVOLVEMENT IN PRODUCTION PROCESS DEVELOPMENT AND IMPROVEMENT QUESTIONNAIRE: SECTION D

Questionnaire Items	Reliability Coefficients (Alphas)[1]/ % of Variance	Factor Loadings[2]
Factor D-1: SUPPLIER INTEGRATION IN PROCESS DEVELOPMENT/IMPROVEMENT OUTCOMES	0.7196 21.1%	
31. Supplier integration into Process Development/Improvement results in reduced-time-to market of new products.		0.7566
32. Supplier integration into Process Development/Improvement results in higher product quality in my Business Unit.		0.6818
34. Suppliers share in cost savings they identify in Process Development/Improvement projects.		0.7830
35. My Business Unit works closely with suppliers to achieve target cost objectives during Process Development/Improvement projects.		0.6692
Factor D-2: OPENNESS TO SUPPLIER INVOLVEMENT IN PROCESS DEVELOPMENT/IMPROVEMENT	0.7171/ 10.9%	
18. Suppliers are used frequently for Process Development/Improvement.		0.8035
22. Supplier efforts are closely coordinated with Process Development/Improvement in my Business Unit.		0.7320
28. Those responsible for Process Development/Improvement in my Business Unit are very receptive to ideas that come from our suppliers.		0.6771
Factor D-3: PROCESS DEVELOPMENT/IMPROVEMENT STRATEGIC EVALUATION	0.8273/ 10.2%	
25. Our Business Unit carefully evaluates whether new process technology is better developed by ourselves or with a supplier.		0.8976
26. Our Business Unit carefully evaluates whether process quality objectives are better met by ourselves or with a supplier.		0.9019

---

[1]Jum C. Nunnally and Ira H. Bernstein, *Psychometric Theory,* 3rd edition (New York: McGraw-Hill, Inc., 1994), pp. 232-233.
[2]Factor Loadings are the correlations between each variable and each factor.

FACTOR ANALYSIS OF PURCHASING INVOLVEMENT IN PRODUCTION PROCESS
DEVELOPMENT AND IMPROVEMENT QUESTIONNAIRE: SECTION D (CONTINUED)

Questionnaire Items	Reliability Coefficients (Alphas)[1]/ % of Variance	Factor Loadings[2]
Factor D-4: STRENGTH OF SUPPLIER SELECTION PROCESS FOR PROCESS DEVELOPMENT/IMPROVEMENT	0.5257/ 8.3%	
27. There must be a high level of familiarity with a supplier's capabilities before the supplier is included in Process Development/Improvement.		0.7611
30. There has to be a strong consensus within our Business Unit before a specific supplier is included in Process Development/Improvement.		0.7388

NOTE: Questionnaire item 29 loaded on factors D-4 and D-6 at >0.500.

Factor D-5: TIMING OF SUPPLIER INVOLVEMENT IN PROCESS DEVELOPMENT/IMPROVEMENT	0.7546/ 6.3%	
20. When used, suppliers become involved in Process Development/Improvement after the concept has been finalized.		0.8215
21. When used, suppliers become involved in Process Development/Improvement after the design has been finalized.		0.8731
Factor D-6: NOT NAMED	NOT APPLICABLE 5.4%	
36. There are on-site supplier personnel in my Business Unit who are assigned full-time to process development/improvement.		
Factor D-7: NOT NAMED	NOT APPLICABLE 5.3%	
33. Suppliers are more likely to be integrated into Process Development/Improvement when the project is technologically complex.		

Total Variance Explained: 62.1%

Questionnaire Item That Loaded on Factors D-4 and D-6 at >0.500:

29. The commitment of our Business Unit's top management is needed to include a specific supplier in Process Development/Improvement.

Questionnaire Items Not Loading on Any Factor:

19. When used, suppliers become involved in Process Development/Improvement at the concept stage.

23. Integration of a supplier into Process Development/Improvement happens only if that supplier's top management is committed.

24. Supplier integration into Process Development/Improvement is carefully controlled in my Business Unit.

---

[1] Jum C. Nunnally and Ira H. Bernstein, *Psychometric Theory,* 3rd edition (New York: McGraw-Hill, Inc., 1994), pp. 232-233.
[2] Factor Loadings are the correlations between each variable and each factor.

Exhibit B-5
FACTOR ANALYSIS OF PURCHASING INVOLVEMENT IN PRODUCTION PROCESS
DEVELOPMENT AND IMPROVEMENT QUESTIONNAIRE: SECTION E

Questionnaire Items	Reliability Coefficients (Alphas)[1]/ % of Variance	Factor Loadings[2]
Factor E-1: BUSINESS UNIT COMPETITIVE RESPONSIVENESS	0.7583/ 42.9%	
37. My Business Unit responds more quickly and effectively to customer or supplier changing needs than do our competition.		0.8460
38. My Business Unit responds more quickly and effectively to changing competitor strategies than does our competitors.		0.8604
39. My Business Unit develops and markets new products more quickly and effectively than our competitors.		0.7023
Factor E-2: COMPETITIVE HOSTILITY	0.6240/ 21.6%	
40. In most of its markets, my Business Unit is a very strong competitor.		0.5126
41. In the markets served by my Business Unit, the firm that eases up usually loses markets/customers to its competitors.		0.8024
42. Competition in the markets served by our Business Unit is severe.		0.8451

Total Variance Explained: 64.6%

---

[1]Jum C. Nunnally and Ira H. Bernstein, *Psychometric Theory,* 3rd edition (New York: McGraw-Hill, Inc., 1994), pp. 232-233.
[2]Factor Loadings are the correlations between each variable and each factor.

Exhibit B-6
PURCHASING INVOLVEMENT IN PRODUCTION PROCESS DEVELOPMENT AND IMPROVEMENT QUESTIONNAIRE: T-TEST OF STUDY FACTORS AND "PROCESS AS A SOURCE OF COMPETITIVE ADVANTAGE"

	Factors	Significance	Means,[1] Process as a Source of Competitive Advantage	
			High >3.97	Low <3.97
B-1	Process as a Source of Competitive Advantage[2]	0.000	4.4188	3.3949
C-1	Purchasing in a Major Process Development/ Improvement Role[3]	0.000	3.8885	3.4438
D-1	Supplier Integration in Process Improvement Outcomes	0.000	3.7846	3.4440
D-2	Openness to Supplier Involvement in Process Development/Improvement[4]	0.000	3.7897	3.4461
D-3	Process Development/Improvement Strategic Evaluation[4]	0.000	3.6115	3.2941
D-5	Timing of Supplier Involvement in Process Development/Improvement[4]	0.063	2.8385	3.0662
E-1	Business Unit Competitive Responsiveness[5]	0.000	3.6023	3.2661
E-2	Competitive Hostility[5]	0.003	4.1389	3.8894

---

[1]Scale for all factors: 1 = Strongly Disagree to 5 = Strongly Agree.
[2]Based on 266 respondents. High = 149, Low = 117.
[3]Based on 219 of 222 respondents who indicated that purchasing participates in Process Development/Improvement. High = 136, Low = 83.
[4]Based on 198 of 203 respondents who indicated that suppliers participate in the Process Development/Improvement Process. High = 130, Low = 68.
[4]Based on 259 of 271 respondents. High = 145, Low = 114.

Exhibit B-7
PURCHASING INVOLVEMENT IN PRODUCTION PROCESS DEVELOPMENT AND IMPROVEMENT
QUESTIONNAIRE: T-TEST OF STUDY FACTORS AND RESPONSES TO QUESTION 9

	Factors	Significance	Means,[1] Does Purchasing Participate in Process Development/ Improvement in Your Business Unit?	
			Yes N=222	No N=49
B-1	Process as a Source of Competitive Advantage[2]	0.000	4.0566	3.5574
D-1	Supplier Integration in Process Development/ Improvement Outcomes[3]	0.008	3.7029	3.3750
D-2	Openness to Supplier Involvement in Process Development/Improvement[3]	0.000	3.7254	3.2564
D-3	Process Development/Improvement Strategic Evaluation[3]	0.607	3.5085	3.4231
D-5	Timing of Supplier Involvement in Process Development/Improvement[3]	0.016	2.8778	3.3077
E-1	Business Unit Competitive Responsiveness[4]	0.220	3.4784	3.3403
E-2	Competitive Hostility[4]	0.319	4.0070	4.1146

[1]Scale: 1 = Strongly Disagree to 5 = Strongly Agree.
[2]Based on 266 of 271 respondents. Yes = 219, No =47.
[3]Based on 201 respondents. Yes = 175, No = 26.
[4]Based on 264 of 271 respondents. Yes = 216, No =48.

PURCHASING INVOLVEMENT IN PRODUCTION PROCESS DEVELOPMENT AND IMPROVEMENT
QUESTIONNAIRE: T-TEST OF STUDY FACTORS AND RESPONSES TO QUESTION 17

| | Factors | Significance | Means,[1] Does Purchasing Participate in Process Development/ Improvement in Your Business Unit? | |
			Yes N=222	No N=49
B-1	Process as a Source of Competitive Advantage[2]	0.000	4.0935	3.5970
C-1	Purchasing in a Major Process Development/ Improvement Role[3]	0.047	3.7778	3.5037
E-1	Business Unit Competitive Responsiveness[4]	0.459	3.4721	3.3980
E-2	Competitive Hostility[4]	0.492	4.0434	3.3980

[1]Scale: 1 = Strongly Disagree to 5 = Strongly Agree.
[2]Based on 268 of 271 respondents. Yes = 199, No = 67.
[3]Based on 222 respondents who indicated that purchasing participates in Process Development/Improvement. Yes = 177, No = 45.
[4]Based on 264 of 271 respondents. Yes = 197, No = 67.

Exhibit B-9
PURCHASING INVOLVEMENT IN PRODUCTION PROCESS DEVELOPMENT AND IMPROVEMENT QUESTIONNAIRE: CONTINGENCY TABLE ANALYSIS OF SELECTED QUESTIONS

1. FOCUS ON PROCESS AS A SOURCE OF COMPETITIVE ADVANTAGE

A.   Process as a Source of Competitive Advantage by Purchasing Participation in Process Development/Improvement

Purchasing Participation in Process Development/ Improvement	Process as a Source of Competitive Advantage		Total
	High	Low	
Yes	136/ (122.7)	83/ (96.3)	219
No	13/ (26.3)	34/ (20.7)	47
Total	149	117	266

Pearson Value = 18.6295, 1 degree of freedom
Significance = 0.0000
Missing Values = 5

B.   Process as a Source of Competitive Advantage by Supplier Participation in Process Development/Improvement

Supplier Participation in Process Development/ Improvement	Process as a Source of Competitive Advantage		Total
	High	Low	
Yes	131/ (111.5)	68/ (87.5)	199
No	18/ (37.5)	49/ (29.5)	
Total	149	117	266

Pearson Value = 30.8854, 1 degree of freedom
Significance = 0.0000
Missing Values = 5

[1]Observed/ (Expected)

PURCHASING INVOLVEMENT IN PRODUCTION PROCESS DEVELOPMENT AND IMPROVEMENT QUESTIONNAIRE: CONTINGENCY TABLE ANALYSIS OF SELECTED QUESTIONS (CONTINUED)

1. FOCUS ON PROCESS AS A SOURCE OF COMPETITIVE ADVANTAGE (CONTINUED)

C. Process as a Source of Competitive Advantage by Industry Category

Industry Category	Process as a Source of Competitive Advantage		Total
	High	Low	
Manufacturing	104/ (94.1)	64/ (73.9)	168
Services	22/ (25.8)	24/ (20.2)	46
Other	23/ (29.1)	29/ (22.9)	52
Total	49	117	266

Pearson Value = 6.5482, 2 degrees of freedom
Significance = 0.0379
Missing Values = 5

D. Process as a Source of Competitive Advantage by Ownership of Business Unit

Ownership of Business Unit	Process as a Source of Competitive Advantage		Total
	High	Low	
United States	129/ (130.5)	104/ (102.5)	233
Other	20/ (18.5)	13/ (14.5)	33
Total	149	117	266

Pearson Value = 0.3223, 1 degree of freedom
Significance = 0.5702
Missing Values = 5

E. Process as a Source of Competitive Advantage by Years of Experience in Purchasing

Years of Experience in Purchasing	Process as a Source of Competitive Advantage		Total
	High	Low	
0 - 10	38/ (35.4)	25/ (27.6)	63
11 or more	111/ (113.6)	91/ (88.4)	202
Total	149	116	265

Pearson Value = 0.5620, 1 degree of freedom
Significance = 0.4535
Missing Values = 6

PURCHASING INVOLVEMENT IN PRODUCTION PROCESS DEVELOPMENT AND IMPROVEMENT
QUESTIONNAIRE: CONTINGENCY TABLE ANALYSIS OF SELECTED QUESTIONS (CONTINUED)

1. FOCUS ON PROCESS AS A SOURCE OF COMPETITIVE ADVANTAGE (CONTINUED)

F.   Process as a Source of Competitive Advantage by Professional Certification

Professional Certification?	Process as a Source of Competitive Advantage		Total
	High	Low	
Yes	70/ (68.1)	52/ (53.9)	122
No	78/ (79.9)	65/ (63.1)	143
Total	148	117	265

Pearson Value = 0.2141, 1 degree of freedom
Significance = 0.6436
Missing Values = 6

PURCHASING INVOLVEMENT IN PRODUCTION PROCESS DEVELOPMENT AND IMPROVEMENT
QUESTIONNAIRE: CONTINGENCY TABLE ANALYSIS OF SELECTED QUESTIONS (CONTINUED)

2. FOCUS ON PURCHASING PARTICIPATION IN PROCESS DEVELOPMENT/IMPROVEMENT

A. Purchasing Participation in Process Development/Improvement by Supplier Participation in Process Development/Improvement

Supplier Participation in Process Development/ Improvement	Purchasing Participation in Process Development/ Improvement		Total
	Yes	No	
Yes	177/ (166.3)	26/ (36.7)	203
No	45/ (55.7)	23/ (12.3)	68
Total	222	49	271

Pearson Value = 15.1884, 1 degree of freedom
Significance = 0.0001
Missing Values = 0

B. Purchasing Participation in Process Development/Improvement by Industry Category

Industry Category	Purchasing Participation in Process Development/ Improvement		Total
	Yes	No	
Manufacturing	142/ (138.4)	27/ (30.6)	169
Services	42/ (38.5)	5/ (8.5)	47
Other	38/ (45.1)	17/ (9.9)	55
Total	222	49	271

Pearson Value = 8.3736, 2 degrees of freedom
Significance = 0.0152
Missing Values = 0

PURCHASING INVOLVEMENT IN PRODUCTION PROCESS DEVELOPMENT AND IMPROVEMENT QUESTIONNAIRE: CONTINGENCY TABLE ANALYSIS OF SELECTED QUESTIONS (CONTINUED)

2. FOCUS ON PURCHASING PARTICIPATION IN PROCESS DEVELOPMENT/IMPROVEMENT (CONTINUED)

C.   Purchasing Participation in Process Development/Improvement by Ownership of the Business Unit

Ownership of Business Unit	Purchasing Participation in Process Development/Improvement		
	Yes	No	Total
United States	195/ (195.0)	43/ (43.0)	238
Other	27/ (27.0)	6/ (6.0)	33
Total	222	49	271

Pearson Value = 0.0003, 1 degree of freedom
Significance = 0.9872
Missing Values = 0

D.   Purchasing Participation in Process Development/Improvement by ears of Experience in Purchasing

Experience in Purchasing	Purchasing Participation in Years of / Process DevelopmentImprovement		
	Yes	No	Total
0 - 10 (51.6)	57/ (11.4)	6/	63
11 or more (169.4)	164/ (37.6)	43/	207
Total	221	49	270

Pearson Value = 4.1146, 1 degree of freedom
Significance = 0.0425
Missing Values = 1

E.   Purchasing Participation in Process Development/Improvement by Professional Certification

Professional Certification?	Purchasing Participation in Process Development/Improvement		
	Yes	No	Total
Yes	98/ (102.3)	27/ (22.7)	125
No	123/ (118.7)	22/ (26.3)	145
Total	221	49	270

Pearson Value = 1.8670, 1 degree of freedom
Significance = 0.1712
Missing Values = 1

PURCHASING INVOLVEMENT IN PRODUCTION PROCESS DEVELOPMENT AND IMPROVEMENT
QUESTIONNAIRE: CONTINGENCY TABLE ANALYSIS OF SELECTED QUESTIONS (CONTINUED)

3. FOCUS ON SUPPLIER PARTICIPATION IN PROCESS DEVELOPMENT/IMPROVEMENT

A. Supplier Participation in Process Development/Improvement by Industry Category

Industry Category	Supplier Participation in Process Development/ Improvement		
	Yes	No	Total
Manufacturing	135/ (126.6)	34/ (42.4)	169
Services	32/ (35.2)	15/ (11.8)	47
Other	36/ (41.2)	19/ (13.8)	55
Total	203	68	271

Pearson Value = 6.0033, 2 degrees of freedom
Significance = 0.0497
Missing Values = 0

B. Supplier Participation in Process Development/Improvement by Ownership of the Business Unit

Ownership of Business Unit	Supplier Participation in Process Development/ Improvement		
	Yes	No	Total
United States	175/ (178.3)	63/ (59.7)	238
Other	28/ (24.7)	5/ (8.3)	33
Total	203	68	271

Pearson Value = 1.9755, 1 degree of freedom
Significance = 0.1599
Missing Values = 0

PURCHASING INVOLVEMENT IN PRODUCTION PROCESS DEVELOPMENT AND IMPROVEMENT QUESTIONNAIRE: CONTINGENCY TABLE ANALYSIS OF SELECTED QUESTIONS (CONTINUED)

3. FOCUS ON SUPPLIER PARTICIPATION IN PROCESS DEVELOPMENT/IMPROVEMENT (CONTINUED)

C. Supplier Participation in Process Development/Improvement by Years of Experience in Purchasing

Years of Experience in Purchasing	Supplier Participation in Process Development/ Improvement		Total
	Yes	No	
0 - 10	48/ (47.1)	15/ (15.9)	63
11 or more	154/ (154.9)	53/ (52.1)	207
Total	202	68	270

Pearson Value = 0.0825, 1 degree of freedom
Significance = 0.7739
Missing Values = 1

D. Supplier Participation in Process Development/Improvement by Professional Certification

Professional Certification?	Supplier Participation in Process Development/ Improvement		Total
	Yes	No	
Yes	97/ (93.5)	28/ (31.5)	125
No	105/ (108.5)	40/ (36.5)	145
Total	202	68	270

Pearson Value = 0.9583, 1 degree of freedom
Significance = 0.3276
Missing Values = 1

APPENDIX V: NARRATIVE INSIGHTS FROM INTERVIEWS •

SUMMARY OF INTERVIEWS: NEW PRODUCT DEVELOPMENT

Nine respondents were interviewed to develop additional insights into the conclusions and findings reported in the executive summary and implications for the practitioner sections of the study. The subjects were selected from those respondents who indicated that their firms' new product success was above average for all individuals responding to the new product development questionnaire, and who provided their name, address, and telephone number in the optional space at the end of the questionnaire. To ensure confidentiality, each respondent is referred to only by the firm's respondent three-digit industry code. Structured telephone interviews were used. The major topics of these interviews were:

- Business unit orientation to time competitiveness
- Thoroughness of evaluation to include suppliers in new product development,
- Purchasing's role in new product development
- Continuing new product commitment by the firm and its suppliers
- Explicit new product development processes
- Sharing of confidential information

Comments about the interviews appear later in this section. In addition, a tenth narrative based on a *Harvard Business Review* article is included. This narrative provides an overview of a method for integrating supplier involvement into the strategic product planning process. The insights developed from these nine interviews are as follows:

1. Business unit orientation to time competitiveness

    All subjects interviewed indicated that time competitiveness was important to their firms. Several respondents indicated that their firms were time competitive. These insights were consistent with the findings from the mail questionnaire.

2. Thoroughness of evaluation to include suppliers in new product development

    All respondents indicated that suppliers involved in new product development were those who had a history of satisfactory performance. Several interviewees indicated that only certified suppliers were included in new product development programs. Overall, the process of selecting suppliers for involvement in new product development is based heavily on past performance with the suppliers under consideration.

    Several respondents did not involve suppliers in new product development. The reasons included (a) a strong internal technological basis for product development, (b) a mature technology that limited supplier involvement to providing samples and quotes, and (c) a dearth of suppliers who were capable of participating meaningfully in new product development.

    The insights gained during the interviews modified the findings of the mail questionnaire by highlighting the importance of past supplier performance, including certification if appropriate, in the decision of whether or not to involve a supplier in new product development.

3. Purchasing's role in new product development

    All nine subjects interviewed indicated that purchasing plays a major role in new product development, regardless of the new product development process, whether or not suppliers are involved. Several of the subjects discussed the necessity of moving purchasing's role beyond that of transaction processing if the potential of purchasing's involvement is to be realized. These insights were consistent with the findings from the mail questionnaire.

4. Continuing new product commitment by the firm and its suppliers, explicit new product development processes, and sharing of confidential information.

    The responses to these issues varied with the level of supplier involvement in new product development. At one end of the spectrum, the interaction between the firm and its suppliers was extensive. This was more likely to occur when supplier involvement provided access to capabilities the firm did not possess. At the other end of the spectrum, the interaction between the firm and its suppliers was minimal. This occurred when the firm had a strong technological base, or when the technology was mature.

These insights amplified the findings of the mail questionnaire by indicating the extent to which supplier involvement in new product development varied among firms, regardless of the level of technology.

SUMMARY OF INTERVIEWS: NEW PROCESS DEVELOPMENT/IMPROVEMENT

Four respondents were interviewed to develop additional insights into the conclusions and findings reported in the executive summary and implications for the practitioner sections of the study. The subjects were selected from those respondents to the process development/improvement questionnaire, who indicated that the strategic importance of process development/improvement to their firms was above average, and who provided their name, address, and telephone number in the optional space at the end of the questionnaire. Structured telephone interviews were conducted. The major topics addressed during these interviews were:

- Business unit orientation to time competitiveness
- Purchasing's role in process development/ improvement
- Process development/improvement strategic evaluation

Detailed comments on the results of these four interviews appear later in this section. The insights developed from these interviews are as follows:

1. Business unit orientation to time competitiveness

   All executives interviewed recognized that process development/improvement plays a major role in improving time competitiveness. This insight is consistent with the results of the mail questionnaire.

2. Purchasing's role in process development/ improvement

   The executives used the terms "major role," "heavily involved," and "from the very beginning" to describe the extent of purchasing's involvement. This is consistent with the results from the mail questionnaire.

3. Process development/improvement strategic evaluation

   The interview subjects revealed that there is a wide range of involvement in process development/ improvement strategic evaluation. The efforts varied from those that have just begun to well developed, multi-staged, comprehensive, cross-functional, interorganizational programs. The range of relationships with suppliers varied from limited to comprehensive. Information sharing and confidentiality agreements were widespread. The responses to the mail questionnaire did not reveal the extent of variation among process development/improvement relationships that was indicated in the interviews.

NEW PRODUCT INTERVIEWS

NEW PRODUCT INTERVIEW #1
INDUSTRY CODE 390 MISCELLANEOUS
MANUFACTURING INDUSTRIES: SCHOOL AND
OFFICE SUPPLIES

Products of this firm are categorized as office/school supplies. Top management is the driving force behind the push for faster new product time to market, increased cross-functional involvement in new product development, and increased supplier involvement in new product development. Management's goal is to reduce product time to market from the current rate of 18 months.

Previously, this firm had been engineering driven, and purchasing's role had been to "rubber stamp" engineering's supplier choices. The coordination among suppliers, engineering, manufacturing, quality control, accounting, and others is currently being funneled through purchasing.

This firm is committed to supplier alliances. In recent years the number of suppliers has decreased from approximately 500 to 120. Formal rating systems are in place for the identification and evaluation of partners. Formal procedures and agreements guide virtually all aspects of supplier partnering and supplier involvement in new product development. Joint buyer-supplier quality training sessions are held at 12 to 18 month intervals.

Suppliers that are partners are routinely included in the new product development process. Time to market and cost objectives are established early in the new product development process and continually reviewed. The participation of supplier partners in new product development programs occurs as a matter of routine. Cross-functional communications between suppliers and the various functions is routine; however, changes in policy must be coordinated through purchasing.

The sharing of confidential technical information, tooling ownership, patent ownership, and customer information is covered by detailed confidentiality agreements. These agreements are developed early in the development of supplier alliances with each partner.

The main problem encountered by the firm as it moved from engineering-focused product development to a team focus was that some individuals had a difficult time giving up their power. In addition, some individuals had difficulty adjusting to a team environment. One unexpected benefit was the amount of cost savings that resulted from the establishment of supplier alliances and supplier involvement in new product development. This purchasing manager felt the increased involvement of suppliers has greatly increased the success of the new product development process.

NEW PRODUCT INTERVIEW #2
INDUSTRY CODE 360 ELECTRIC/ELECTRONIC EQUIPMENT: COMPUTER MASS STORAGE HARDWARE

This firm markets proprietary software and hardware for mass storage of computer data. According to the purchaser interviewed, this firm maintains a two-year lead over its competition. The source of competition is (a) adapting off-the-shelf components furnished by suppliers and (b) designing circuit boards and cabinets that are produced by contract manufacturers. Operations at this firm focus on final assembly and testing of finished product.

The products of this firm interface with customer computer systems in the banking, airlines reservations, and health care industries. As a result, this firm strives to avoid product designs that are different from industry norms.

Supplier involvement in new product development occurs in two ways. First, the firm maintains a close relationship with suppliers to identify the development of off-the-shelf components that will provide the needed performance for new products. This monitoring of supplier products is continuous and interactive. The current and future needs of the customers must be matched to supplier's current and future components. The firm's focus is on identifying standard items that will fit into its product line.

Second, the firm designs its own proprietary circuit boards and cabinets. The circuit boards and cabinets are based on property hardware and software technology that provide the firm with its source of competitive advantage. Both circuit boards and cabinets are produced by contract manufacturers. The firm provides the contract manufacturers with the designs, the contract manufacturers offer suggestions regarding design changes, and the firm finalizes its requirements.

Suppliers are not intimately involved with the development of property technology and hardware. Needs and capabilities are exchanged over a wide range of technical and market considerations. Confidential information is shared as needed and protected by formal confidentiality agreements.

This firm maximizes supplier involvement in new product development by focusing on items that are readily available (or will soon be available) on the market,

focusing its creative efforts on the specific software and hardware technology that will provide its competitive advantage, subcontracting the manufacture of propriety components, and focusing its operational efforts on final assembly and testing.

NEW PRODUCT INTERVIEW #3
INDUSTRY CODE 730 BUSINESS SERVICES

The purchasing professional interviewed belongs to an information technology company that offers service support to banking and credit card businesses.

Purchasing plays a lead role in the organization as the firm's sole point of contact for all its suppliers. No formalized system exists to select suppliers; however, internal cross-functional teams are formed when necessary to select suppliers.

The company enters into long-term contracts with key suppliers. These contracts often include agreements on guaranteed pricing, reliability, quality, and quantity. The company has cut the total number of suppliers, and the remaining few are forced to remain competitive. The firm is committed to its suppliers with permanent on-site co-location of supplier personnel. Even though there are no shared physical assets, there are formal risk-reward sharing agreements. Successful new product development requires some sharing of technological information and customer requirements.

NEW PRODUCT INTERVIEW #4
INDUSTRY CODE 390 MANUFACTURED HOUSING AND RECREATIONAL VEHICLES

This firm is a major producer of manufactured housing (permanent housing manufactured off site) and recreational vehicles (motor homes). It manufactures over 50,000 homes per year at over 20 locations nationally. This interview focused on the manufactured housing aspect of the business because it is much larger than the recreational vehicle business and uses a more advanced new product development process. The firm will eventually apply new product development techniques developed for manufactured housing to recreational vehicles.

This firm's commitment to time competitiveness was driven by top management's commitment to computer assisted drafting (CAD) and cross-functional teams. The use of CAD enables designers to revise and cost design changes much faster than is possible with manual design techniques. Cross-functional teams, ingrained into the organization by top management, capitalize on the information provided by CAD to evaluate trade-offs in new product design features. The implementation of cross-functional teams was a major change in this firm. It required that the employee performance measurement process be changed to reflect the importance of team participation.

Supplier involvement in new product development requires a high degree of trust and commitment by the supplier throughout its organization. A few suppliers are in tune with the process, but many suppliers, "Talk a good game but do not walk the talk." According to this purchaser, supplier involvement in new product development only works when the supplier is structured to participate. Too often the sales representative's promises and interest are not supported by the supplier's internal organization.

Purchasing plays a key role in the early involvement in new product development, provides leadership in cross-functional teams, and identifies suppliers that offer competitive technology. A core group of seasoned employees run the team processes. Teams form and disband as needed, and the most critical characteristic of these teams is representation from across the organization. Team performance is always evaluated.

The major change for purchasing has been to become proficient in team involvement. Before this change could occur, purchasing was reengineered to reduce the paper flow and move away from its transaction orientation.

Suppliers are involved in new product development to the extent that they add value. For example, one tool supplier has worked closely with this firm to develop processes for reducing the number of labor hours needed for nailing. This involved close cooperation and included many ad hoc meetings to exchange ideas.

While this purchasing executive feels that the firm has become genuinely open to ideas from outsiders, many salespeople do not get the necessary technical support from their firms to meaningfully participate in new product development. In most cases, suppliers that are involved in new product development are large national firms with an understanding of the importance of multi-organizational cross-functional teams.

Confidential agreements are commonly used to enable this firm to capitalize on new ideas applicable to new product development, product improvement, and improved processes. Depending on the buying firm's contributions, purchasing negotiates for exclusivity or royalties. When the development expenses are borne by the supplier, exclusive use of the material, or process, for approximately six months is sought. If development costs are borne by the buyer, royalties and exclusivity are sought.

NEW PRODUCT INTERVIEW #5
INDUSTRY CODE 200 FOOD AND KINDRED PRODUCTS

This purchasing executive is employed by a regional fast-food chain with over 1,000 restaurants. Product time-to-market and responsiveness to competitor actions are about the same as in other firms in the industry. The interview subject stated that responsiveness to changing customer needs has been improving but did not know how this firm compares to its competitors. According to the interview subject "Marketing drives everything." Top management has a strong marketing orientation.

An extensive formal process is used to qualify suppliers. Qualified suppliers are included in new product development informally, with little additional evaluation. Supplier involvement in new product development emphasizes four areas: (1) new technology, (2) new raw materials, (3) new operational equipment, and (4) refine ingredient and process operational friendliness. This firm works closely with its suppliers in the new product process, especially in the achievement of target cost objectives.

New product development teams, called task forces, include representatives from marketing, purchasing, quality assurance, and operational services. Purchasing's role includes early involvement, active participation in task forces, and the identification of suppliers that offer competitive technology. There are few problems with task forces in this firm; they have been used for a long time and any problems in adapting to a team approach were resolved years ago.

Many issues of buyer-supplier new product development commitment are addressed during supplier certification. Shared training, co-location of personnel, and sharing of physical assets occasionally occur with strategic suppliers. Formalized risk-reward agreements are not used.

The new product development process is formal. The initial supplier certification process establishes relationship ground rules that will guide supplier involvement in new product development.

Policies concerning the sharing of confidential information are included in the supplier certification process. The ownership of patents and other rights resulting from supplier involvement in new product development are largely determined by the level of each party's investment.

NEW PRODUCT INTERVIEW #6
INDUSTRY CODE 390 MISCELLANEOUS
MANUFACTURING: BICYCLES

The purchasing manager interviewed belongs to a bicycle assembling business. The firm assembles bicycles from parts imported mostly from Japan and Taiwan.

The firm provides incentives to support time competitiveness by offering profit sharing to its employees. One main obstacle to time competitiveness is the long lead-time required to source supplies from oversees. The supplies arrive by sea; as a result, production has to be locked in for 3 to 6 months. The firm is trying to speed up sourcing through the use of EDI and e-mail.

The question of whether or not to use suppliers is not an issue for the firm because they are assemblers with no production of their own. They use a small group of suppliers and, based on their performance over the years on parameters like quality and timely delivery, these suppliers have been given repeat business.

There is no partnering of any sort. Occasionally, the suppliers are asked to develop products to the firm's specifications, but with no inputs from the supplier side. There is some exchange of confidential information, but this is covered by confidentiality agreements.

NEW PRODUCT INTERVIEW #7
INDUSTRY CODE 360 ELECTRIC/ELECTRONIC
EQUIPMENT: COMMUNICATIONS EQUIPMENT

This organization is a large producer of communications equipment supported by a large research organization. According to the purchasing executive, the organization is better at product innovation than at product implementation. Management determines the goals, and the results come from the middle-level managers and researchers.

Purchasing is involved in major new product development at an early stage. Purchasing becomes involved in product redesign/modification programs later in the development process, usually after the design has been finalized. Cross-functional teams are used as needed. Purchasing's role in these teams is to provide leadtime input and "slow down or speed-up the thinking."

Technical staff are free to talk to suppliers but are not permitted to initiate buying commitments. An important role of purchasing is to remain informed of these discussions in order to avoid any surprises resulting from supplier or technical personnel creating premature expectations of future sales.

Supplier involvement in new product development tends to be passive. Supplier input into product quality and cost improvements are constantly sought; however, suppliers are usually involved in new product development at the development stage. Supplier involvement usually does not occur until after the concept has been finalized, usually just before or after design finalization. Supplier involvement is greater in revised products. In addition, suppliers play an active role in product redesign and improvement.

As a result of the lack of supplier involvement in new product development in this firm, there is very little interaction in the areas of shared training, shared physical assets, co-location of personnel, and formalized risk-reward agreements.

Technical information is shared on an as-needed basis. This firm usually tries to buy any technical rights associated with new product development projects.

NEW PRODUCT INTERVIEW #8
INDUSTRY CODE 500 WHOLESALE TRADE:
DURABLE GOODS

This firm is an electronics distributor with over $200,000 in annual sales. Competitive in its markets, the product line focuses on components used in printed circuit boards. Product development emphasizes finding sources of electronic components that meet customer needs. New product development focuses on developing operational responses to specific requirements and does not include substantial amounts of engineering, design, development, or coordination among functional units. Coordination with suppliers consists of bringing in two or three major suppliers to identify components with the necessary features and then coordinating package design with a major packaging materials supplier.

Purchasing is responsible for identifying suppliers and working with packaging vendors. Purchasing's charge is to call suppliers to develop a response to the task at hand, develop cost figures, and then present this information to the chief financial officer.

Relations with suppliers are informal with little in the way of continuing cooperation and coordination. There is little activity in the areas of shared training and education, co-location of personnel, sharing of physical assets, and formalized risk-reward agreements.

While this firm is ISO 9002 certified, new product development processes are adequately addressed in the procedures for buying, repackaging, selling, and shipping electronics components. There is little exchange of confidential information between the firm and its suppliers.

NEW PRODUCT INTERVIEW #9
INDUSTRY CODE 340 FABRICATED METAL
PRODUCTS

This firm manufactures expanded metal, welded bar gratings, and metal lath. These products are used in a wide range of industrial and consumer applications including outdoor lawn furniture, industrial equipment guards, interior and exterior wall finishing, and industrial flooring.

This firms's competitive responsiveness was summarized as about average, slower than some competitors but faster than others.

Suppliers play a major role in new product development. This role focuses on capacity planning, cost, and material availability. Within the range of this focus, the firm coordinates closely with suppliers, working to achieve availability and cost objectives.

New product development is sequential and informal. Marketing develops new product ideas, engineering designs the product, and marketing provides the raw material. Cross-functional coordination is minimal, according to the purchasing executive interviewed, because of the straightforward nature of the business.

NEW PRODUCT NARRATIVE #10
CUMMINS ENGINE COMPANY

This narrative is based on the article "Strategic Sourcing: To Make or Not To Make" that appeared in the November-December 1992 issue of the Harvard Business Review. Cummins Engine managers were not interviewed for this narrative. The article presents an approach to determining whether a specific item should be developed and produced without supplier participation, developed and produced with supplier participation, or outsourced.

A central component of Cummins' approach is the identification of the key technology and capabilities needed to specify, design, and manufacture a specific component, such as pistons. Next was the identification of the rates of learning in the key technology and capabilities.

The foundation of the strategic sourcing process is the understanding of linkages among user requirements, system parameters, and component specifications. How the product is going to be differentiated? How good are we compared to our competitors? Can we become/stay world class? Ultimately, the key is not in buying or making specific components. Rather, it is developing the ability to preserve architectural knowledge, whether or not a specific item is made or bought.

According to the article, Cummins focuses on ability, investment, and cost. If the family of components is strategic, the design and process capabilities are available, and the costs to become/stay in a position of leadership are justified, then the decision should be to focus, invest, and become/stay world class. If the investment is too great, then the decision is to outsource but maintain control of the architecture.

If the components are not strategic, the focus will be on immediate outsourcing, gradual harvesting, or providing the opportunity for internal producers to become competitive.

Overall, this article provides an extensive framework for the question of strategic sourcing. The extent of supplier involvement will depend on the detailed analysis of Cummins' needs, capabilities, investment requirements, and costs. Regardless of the level of supplier involvement, the need to maintain control over the design and manufacture is critical if critical advantage is to be maintained.

This article provides a methodology for ascertaining the level of supplier involvement. According to this article, the level of supplier involvement in new product development is secondary to maintaining the knowledge base to control the design and manufacture of the product.

PROCESS DEVELOPMENT/IMPROVEMENT INTERVIEWS

PROCESS DEVELOPMENT/IMPROVEMENT
INTERVIEW #1
350 MACHINERY, EXCEPT ELECTRICAL

This firm manufactures pumps for the petroleum and chemical industries. This industry is mature. A program of supplier involvement in process development/improvement began recently. According to the purchasing executive interviewed, there is not a lot of history to judge the success of the program, but the researchers feel it will meet or exceed expectations. Initial efforts focus on major costs which are motors, casting, and seals.

Purchasing plays a major role in supplier involvement in process development/improvement, coordinating efforts among suppliers, accounting, engineering, sales and purchasing.

The purchasing executive interviewed reported there have been no significant problems implementing the process. According to this executive, "Everyone has been pretty much receptive and recognize that this is not just an overnight process." In a word of caution, the executive states, "You need to be realistic with whom you partner with. Every supplier is not able to make the time and effort commitments that are required to be involved in our process improvement program."

Openness to supplier involvement has increased, and suppliers are being used increasingly in process development/improvement. Decisions of whether or not to use suppliers for specific projects are made informally at this time.

PROCESS DEVELOPMENT/IMPROVEMENT
INTERVIEW #2
300 HIGH PRESSURE PLASTIC LAMINATE

The purchasing professional belongs to the high pressure plastic laminate industry. The main product is formica used in table tops.

The interview subject feels that the firm is not competitive enough in terms of new process development due to a lacking design staff. The firm is trying to correct this situation. On the other hand, the firm is ahead of its competitors in terms of leadtime for the development of existing processes. This is possible due to their competence in manufacturing and chemistry.

Purchasing is involved in new process development from the very beginning. Working with cross-functional teams, purchasing plays a major part in the purchase of equipment as well as process technology. Decentralized purchasing personnel are used for improved effectiveness.

There is a formal system in place for deciding whether or not to use suppliers in new process development as well as selecting suppliers from the qualified pool. It is a four stage go no-go system which helps determine which supplier will stay and which will be dropped.

The relationship between the firm and its suppliers is not one of partnering but rather that of strategic alliances. There is not much of risk-reward sharing; however, incentives such as bonuses and repeat business are in place to reward on-time completion of projects and delivery of equipment. There is not much sharing of confidential information on technology or customers.

PROCESS DEVELOPMENT/IMPROVEMENT
INTERVIEW #3
200 FOOD AND KINDRED PRODUCTS

The respondent felt that time competitiveness is critical to the business. The firm belongs to the franchise bottling industry and is ahead of the competition in terms of reducing lead and cycle times.

Purchasing plays a key role in new process development by being involved in capital equipment investment decisions and their design, development, and installation.

Purchasing is also a part of the cross-functional team that regularly scouts for valuable process improvements from their suppliers. They help in quantifying the value of any potential process improvement and in qualifying the suppliers.

A formal system for selecting suppliers is evolving but, being a franchise, there is limitation to the freedom in selecting suppliers.

Information is shared with suppliers on a confidential basis. There are no shared physical assets. Deals and expenditures are structured so as to reward participation by the supplier. Better performance on the supplier side is usually rewarded with long-term business.

PROCESS DEVELOPMENT/IMPROVEMENT #4
390 PHARMACEUTICAL

This respondent from a pharmaceutical industry felt the biggest obstacle to time competitiveness was getting products approved by the FDA. Being time competitive in this industry is tied to process development performance.

Purchasing is "heavily" involved in new process development, from discovery to lab to pilot to scale, up to manufacturing integration. There is a system in place to select suppliers. Researchers can immediately access an approved list of suppliers, which is online. The suppliers can then be matched to the required technology or process.

In return for proprietary process technology, the suppliers are awarded multi-year contracts that allow them to recoup their investments and spread their expenditures. Exchanges of critical information are covered under multi-party confidential disclosure agreements that may include third-parties.

CENTER FOR ADVANCED PURCHASING STUDIES •

THE **CENTER FOR ADVANCED PURCHASING STUDIES (CAPS)** was established in November 1986 as the result of an affiliation agreement between the College of Business at Arizona State University and the National Association of Purchasing Management. It is located at The Arizona State University Research Park, 2055 East Centennial Circle, P.O. Box 22160, Tempe, Arizona 85285-2160 (Telephone [602] 752-2277).

The Center has three major goals to be accomplished through its research program:

to improve purchasing effectiveness and efficiency;
to improve overall purchasing capability;
to increase the competitiveness of U.S. companies in a global economy.

Research published includes 26 focus studies on purchasing/materials management topics ranging from purchasing organizational relationships to CEOs' expectations of the purchasing function, as well as benchmarking reports on purchasing performance in 26 industries.

Research under way includes: *Early Supplier Involvement in New Product Design; Developing Internet Electronic Commerce Strategies for Purchasing and Supply Chain Management; Environmental Scan for Purchasing and Supply Management;* and the benchmarking reports of purchasing performance by industry.

CAPS, affiliated with two 501 (c) (3) educational organizations, is funded solely by tax-deductible contributions from organizations and individuals who want to make a difference in the state of purchasing and materials management knowledge. Policy guidance is provided by the Board of Trustees consisting of: